Easy
Compost

Niall Dunne
Editor

Beth Hanson
Editor, 1997 Edition

BROOKLYN
BOTANIC GARDEN

Elizabeth Peters
DIRECTOR OF DIGITAL
AND PRINT MEDIA

Sarah Schmidt
SENIOR EDITOR

Susan Pell
Craig Cogger
SCIENCE EDITORS

Joni Blackburn
COPY EDITOR

Elizabeth Ennis
ART DIRECTOR

Scot Medbury
PRESIDENT

Elizabeth Scholtz
DIRECTOR EMERITUS

Handbook #199

Copyright © 2013 by Brooklyn Botanic Garden, Inc.

ISBN 978-1-889538-84-6

Printed in China by Ocean Graphics Press.

♻ Printed with soy-based inks on
postconsumer recycled paper.

Guides for a Greener Planet are published by
Brooklyn Botanic Garden, 1000 Washington Avenue,
Brooklyn, NY 11225.

Learn more at bbg.org/handbooks.

Cover: What's not to love about compost? Above: By composting our food scraps, we return organic matter to the earth, where it is beneficial, instead of burying it in a landfill, where it contributes to pollution and other environmental problems.

Easy Compost

Introduction

Niall Dunne

Farmers and gardeners have long understood the benefits of compost to their soil and plants. An annual application of compost enhances soil's structure and its ability to hold water. It also creates habitat for beneficial soil organisms, provides a source of slow-release nutrients for plants, and protects plants from soil-borne pathogens. Though the process of making compost hasn't changed much over time, more and more people are becoming interested in the key role composting plays in soil conservation, sustainable plant care, and the reduction of organic waste. No longer confined to rural and agricultural areas, composting is now regularly practiced in the heart of our cities, too, by green thumbs in high-rise apartments, community gardens, and schoolyard horticulture programs.

Easy Compost was first published in 1997, and this revised edition remains an essential guide to the science and art of composting. It explains how composting benefits your garden as well as the larger environment and describes the role of earthworms and other tiny creatures that turn your kitchen scraps and garden clippings into "black gold." At the heart of the book are the basics of what you need to know to make good compost: which materials to include, where to locate your pile, what type of bin to use, troubleshooting tips, and instructions for composting indoors. You'll also find brand-new chapters on compost tea; vermicomposting in schools; urban composting, including profiles of five innovative community composting sites in Brooklyn; and an expanded guide for building your own composter.

In an age of anxiety over climate change, air and water pollution, biodiversity loss, and the increasing threat of ecosystem collapse, composting is more crucial than it has ever been before. By enabling homeowners and gardeners to recycle their own waste, cut down on irrigation needs, and reduce their dependence on fossil-fuel-based fertilizers and pesticides, composting offers people a way to significantly lessen their environmental impact and grow plants more sustainably. Composting is also easy and fun, so that everyone—from kids to grown-ups—can get involved and live more in harmony with nature.

In New York City, almost one third of the waste stream could be composted. Here and around the country, citizens and municipalities are finding ways to make that happen.

Why Compost?
Grace Gershuny

Compost is a key component of modern organic and sustainable plant care. It can enhance growing conditions in your home garden by nurturing beneficial soil organisms, improving soil aeration and water-holding capacity, providing a modest source of plant nutrients, and protecting plants against pests and diseases. Since the raw materials of compost—kitchen scraps and yard clippings—would otherwise be disposed of as garbage, the act of composting also provides a significant environmental benefit by diverting huge amounts of organic waste from our overburdened landfills. In addition, compost can save money by helping to cut down on or eliminate the costs of watering, fertilizing, and controlling pests. And you'll be happy to know that you don't need a degree in soil science to make the stuff. In fact, we humans have been using compost to enrich our soils and improve the health of our garden plants for millennia.

Nurturing the Soil Food Web

Compost is the product of the controlled aerobic decomposition of organic matter by microbes and other organisms. Making it in your backyard or at a municipal facility mimics and accelerates the natural decomposition processes that occur in forests and grasslands when plants die and are consumed by bacteria, fungi, and other members of the soil food web. Finished compost is made up mostly of humus, a stable organic matter that is relatively resistant to further decay. This dark, spongy, earthy-smelling substance works wonders for soil's physical structure and chemistry, as well as its biological health. Soil with plenty of humus has a good mix of air and moisture, which most soil organisms—and plants—need to thrive.

Most compost also contains active organic matter that can still be decomposed. This food source supports a rich diversity of soil microbes and invertebrates. As these decomposers break down the organic matter, they release nutrients into the soil, making them available for absorption by plant roots.

Composting is easy and fun and helps us make our gardens and our planet healthier and more sustainable in significant ways.

Promoting Good Tilth

Soil that has good physical qualities is said to be in good tilth. This means that it has optimal structure, readily allows both air and water to enter, and retains enough of each to meet the needs of its inhabitants. (Most soil organisms and plants need a balanced mix of air and water to survive.) Soil in good tilth is easy to work using garden tools and allows roots to penetrate easily. It resists erosion, retains water in time of drought, and holds enough air to prevent plants from drowning when it rains heavily. Although many people think first of plant nutrients when considering soil fertility, tilth is at least as important—many fertility problems can be helped more by improving structure than by adding fertilizers.

Soil structure refers to the properties of soil components—clay, silt, sand, and particles of organic matter—as a mass, or aggregate. Good-quality soil has a granular or crumbly structure containing a balance of large pores, which allow water to infiltrate, drain down, and be replaced by air, and small pores, which absorb and retain moisture. The essential ingredient for creating and maintaining good crumb structure is organic matter, which in average soil is between 50 and 80 percent humus. It binds soil particles together and provides food for soil organisms whose activities and secretions further stabilize granular aggregates.

Using compost is the best way to deliver humus-rich organic matter to your garden soil and promote good structure. Compost is the supreme soil conditioner. It increases infiltration and permeability in heavy-textured clay soils and compacted soils and makes them easier to work. In light-textured sandy soils, compost helps retain moisture, reduce erosion, and prevent soluble nutrients from leaching away.

Fertilizing Soil Over Time

Compost not only conditions soil but also acts as a slow-release plant fertilizer. Compared with synthetic fertilizers, compost generally has a low concentration of the primary nutrients nitrogen, phosphorus, and potassium. However, unlike synthetics, it releases those nutrients gradually over time.

This has many advantages. Whereas highly soluble synthetic fertilizers can easily dissolve in rainwater and wash away from the garden—also threatening the health of nearby groundwater—nutrients provided gradually by compost are taken up by plants as they become available, so they aren't wasted. In addition, highly soluble fertilizers make excessive amounts of nutrients available, and plants may take up more nutrients than they need. Excess nitrogen in particular creates overly lush, watery growth that is more susceptible to attack by pests and diseases. (Too much compost could potentially lead to nutrient excesses in soil, but this is rare. See "Using Compost in the Garden," page 81, for compost application rates.)

In addition to being a source of major plant nutrients, compost contains a mix of micronutrients, or trace elements, such as iron and zinc, essential players in the

Compost adds nutrients to the soil and stores them so that plants may take them up when they are needed. It also unlocks nutrients trapped in very acidic or alkaline soil.

molecular interactions on which all living organisms—including people—depend. You can provide plants with other sources of these nutrients, but the safest and most reliable way to provide them is by adding compost. Plants need only tiny amounts of micronutrients, and too much of any of them can be harmful. Living tissue generally contains a good balance of micronutrients, so when it is composted, its nutrients are made available in just the right proportions to feed new organisms.

Holding Nutrients for Use by Plants

Nutrients that plants need can be stored efficiently with the help of the colloids—insoluble, negatively charged particles—in humus. Positively charged nutrients, including calcium, magnesium, potassium, and several important micronutrients, are held at these colloidal exchange sites, where they stay available for plants.

Humus molecules also bind plant nutrients into chemical complexes in a process called chelation, which prevents them from being washed away by water percolating down through the soil yet makes them readily usable by plants and microbes. This same mechanism also helps detoxify soil if it is overdosed with essential nutrients, and even when it has been contaminated with toxic heavy metals such as lead or cadmium.

Finally, although plants get most of the carbon they need from the air in the form of carbon dioxide, the organic matter in finished compost is also an important

Environmental Benefits of Compost

- Reduces contributions to the municipal waste stream
- Reduces the need for synthetic fertilizers and pesticides
- Conserves water by reducing irrigation needs
- Sequesters atmospheric carbon dioxide in soil as stable humus
- Binds with pollutants, preventing them from running off into the groundwater

Soil Benefits of Compost

- Increases populations of earthworms and other beneficial creatures
- Promotes a healthy microbial population
- Improves soil structure
- Reduces compaction
- Improves soil aeration and water retention
- Helps to form soil aggregates
- Slowly releases macronutrients
- Increases nutrient-holding capacity
- Increases nutrient availability
- Adds micronutrients
- Moderates pH levels
- Supresses soil-borne pests and diseases
- Decreases thatch
- Ties up heavy metals

source of carbon for plants, as well as for other organisms living in the soil. As it decomposes, carbon dioxide is released near the soil surface, close to where plants are growing, and can significantly stimulate growth.

Unlocking Additional Nutrients

Compost also helps stimulate the release of additional nutrients already present in soil but in forms unavailable to plants. Their availability is strongly influenced by the soil's acidity or alkalinity. The slightly acid pH of 6.5 is ideal for most plants. Problems result when the soil pH is either too low (strongly acidic, pH 3.5 to 5.5) or too high (strongly alkaline, pH 8 to 10). Very acid soils often have low amounts of soluble potassium, phosphorus, and calcium and can release excess micronutrients and aluminum in levels that are harmful to plants. In strongly alkaline soil, the nutrients phosphorus, iron, copper, and zinc are often locked up in insoluble forms. Humus moderates both low and high pH, a quality known as buffering, and so improves the availability of nutrients in both acidic and alkaline soils.

Compost also works biologically to improve nutrient availability. Soil microbes are most active and diverse when soil pH is close to neutral (pH 6 to 7). The diverse population of microbes in compost goes to work on decay-resistant organic materials, unlocking plant nutrients such as phosphorus. Furthermore, certain kinds of fungi form symbiotic relationships with plant roots, exchanging phosphorus taken up by the fungi for carbohydrates produced by the plants in a process called mycorrhiza.

Fighting Pests and Diseases

The value of compost goes beyond improving soil structure and providing nutrients. Soil health is, as we've seen, directly related to plant health. And, as is true of healthy people, healthy plants are better able to resist attack by pests and disease-causing pathogens. The right balance of nutrients, released at the rate at which they are needed by plants, helps prevent disease and insect problems, such as those caused by excess nitrogen.

Compost also works directly to protect plants from soil-borne pathogens by inoculating them with organisms that fight disease. It is no accident that most antibiotics are derived from microorganisms that can be found in healthy soil. Compost tea, made by steeping compost in water (see "Compost Tea for the Home Gardener," page 86), has also been found to prevent certain fungal diseases like mildew, and researchers are now able to produce custom composts that can suppress specific disease-causing organisms such as *Pythium* species, fungi that cause root rot and kill seeds and seedlings before or as they emerge from cool, wet soils.

Providing Environmental Benefits

Compost is the closest thing possible to a garden elixir, replenishing the life in your soil and keeping your plants in good health. But if that weren't enough, compost offers great benefits to the environment at large. Most obviously, composting can divert enormous amounts of waste from our overburdened landfills and recycle it into a useful soil amendment for gardens and farms. According to the U.S. Environmental Protection Agency, food scraps and yard clippings make up between 20 to 30 percent of our current waste stream and should be composted. Furthermore, when this organic waste is buried in a landfill, it decomposes anaerobically, releasing methane—a potent greenhouse gas with 21 times the climate change potential of carbon dioxide. Compost provides numerous other benefits to the environment, such as reducing the need for water, fertilizers, and pesticides on farms and landscapes and serving as a low-cost way to remediate contaminated soils.

Compost and the Soil Food Web

Benjamin Grant

A visit to any backyard compost heap will yield a wide variety of visible decomposers. In a healthy pile, earthworms, sowbugs, millipedes, centipedes, mites, springtails, and beetles abound. Molds and other fungi, along with long white strands of funguslike actinomycetes, often sprout from the rotting material. The real action, however, is happening at the microscopic level. Billions of invisible bacteria, fungi, and other microorganisms consume the organic material in short order, breaking it down and releasing nutrients.

The members of this astonishingly diverse group of living things not only feed on the organic matter, they also interact with one another. Centipedes, for example, are predators, feeding on a variety of insects and then enriching the pile with their castings. Scavengers like sowbugs and snails break apart rotting matter, exposing more surface area and allowing microorganisms to move in. Earthworms depend on bacteria to soften up material before they consume it, and their burrowing helps aerate the pile, enhancing conditions for microbes. All this activity takes place in a moist medium full of enzymes, sugars, and nutrients, all of biological origin. Where there is decomposition, there is a complex ecosystem at work.

Recipe for Compost

- Organic matter
- Decomposers
- Room for decomposers to work
- Air (oxygen)
- Moisture (water)
- Time

Encouraging Aerobic Decomposition

As in all ecosystems, the organisms in a compost pile thrive under certain specific conditions. Successful composting is simply a matter of maintaining the appropriate habitat for the decomposers. The most desirable decomposers take in oxygen and use it to break down sugars for energy, releasing carbon dioxide and water. This is called aerobic metabolism.

Among the decomposers you might find in your backyard compost pile are (clockwise from top left): a springtail, a sowbug, mites, an earthworm with springtails, a ground beetle, a centipede, a pseudoscorpion, and a snail.

As single-celled organisms, bacteria cannot ingest complex materials, so much of their digestion must take place in the liquid medium that surrounds them. They accomplish this "extracellular" digestion by secreting digestive enzymes into the solution, then taking up simple sugars that the enzymes break out of more complex materials. That's why a moist habitat is essential for most bacteria.

Though decomposers depend on water, there can be too much of a good thing. A wet, mucky environment allows very little air to circulate, and anaerobic bacteria, which can decompose organic matter without oxygen, take over. These bacteria are much less efficient in the compost pile, and the by-products of their efforts can include ammonia, sulfide gases, and alcohols—which smell awful. The anaerobic process is better suited to swamps, where it occurs naturally, than to backyards, where it is quite avoidable.

Besides air and water, the ideal habitat for decomposers contains an appropriate balance of nutrients—in particular, carbon and nitrogen. Carbon forms the backbone of organic compounds required by bacteria and other microbes for energy and growth, and nitrogen is needed to make proteins and genetic material. Getting a good nutrient balance is simple enough—just remember to compose your pile of a roughly even mix of nitrogen-rich "greens" such as grass clippings, kitchen scraps, and garden clippings, and carbon-rich "browns" like fall leaves and newspaper. (See "Basic Ingredients and Techniques," page 18.)

To a large extent, creating a good compost pile involves replicating a typical forest floor, where fallen leaves and other organic matter break down into humus naturally over time.

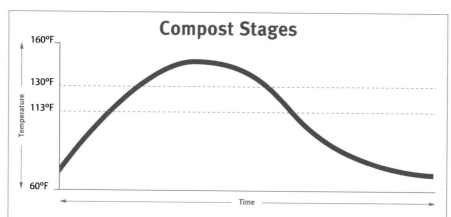

Compost Stages

Mesophilic Phase
68°F to 113°F

Initially, mesophilic bacteria and fungi—those organisms that thrive in moderate heat—reign. As they break down sugars, they give off heat, which will cause the temperature of the compost pile to rise.

Thermophilic Phase
113°F and up

Thermophilic organisms take over and break down proteins, fats, and complex carbohydrates like cellulose. If the pile reaches 130°F or above, pathogens and weed seeds are killed. Eventually, the organisms that thrive at these temperatures deplete their food sources. Decomposition slows, and the temperature of the pile begins to drop.

Curing Phase
Decomposition slows

During this phase, mesophilic organisms—including actinomycetes, which give compost its earthy smell—take over again, continuing the slow decomposition of lignin and other tough compounds. Compost may be ready to use anywhere from two weeks to six months after this final temperature drop.

Composting Phases

If the balance of nutrients, water, and air is just right, microbial activity really takes off. Under these optimal conditions, composting proceeds in three distinct phases, dominated by different types of microorganisms. Initially, at temperatures of 68°F to 113°F, mesophilic (moderate heat–loving) bacteria and fungi get to work breaking down readily digestible organic compounds. As these microorganisms consume sugars, they give off some of the sugars' energy as heat. With enough activity and a large enough pile, heat will start to accumulate and the temperature will rise.

Composting's second stage occurs after the temperature in a pile rises to about 113°F, when mesophilic organisms become less competitive and new, thermophilic (high heat–loving) bacteria thrive. Thermophilic organisms break down complex molecules such as proteins and fats and complex carbohydrates like cellulose. After their work is done and food sources are depleted, they die off, decomposition slows, and the temperature of the pile drops.

Organisms in the Compost Food Web

Primary consumers: Organisms that feed directly on organic matter

Examples: Actinomycetes and other bacteria; mold, and other fungi

Role: to break up organic matter

Higher-level consumers: Organisms that eat primary consumers and each other

Examples: springtails, nematodes, protozoa, centipedes, pseudoscorpions, snails, slugs, spiders, mites, beetles, earthworms

Roles: to keep populations of primary consumers and each other in check, to enrich the compost pile with their excretions, and to aerate the compost as they move through it

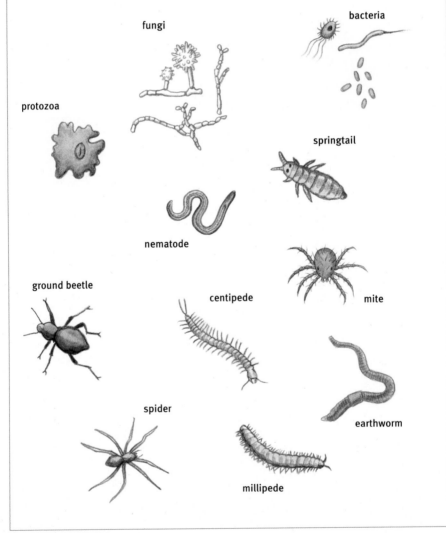

fungi

bacteria

protozoa

springtail

nematode

ground beetle

centipede

mite

spider

millipede

earthworm

During the final stage, mesophilic organisms—including the actinomycetes, which give compost its pleasant earthy smell—take over to "cure" the compost, continuing the slow decomposition of lignin (a complex polymer that imparts mechanical strength to wood) and other tough-to-break-down organic compounds. Compost may be ready to use anywhere from two weeks to six months after this final temperature drop, though in general, the longer the maturation or curing phase, the more diverse the final microbial community will be.

Temperatures in the best-managed "hot"—fast-decomposing—backyard pile get up to around 130°F. Hot composting offers a way to kill soil pathogens and weed seeds. Most composting facilities make sure to maintain an interior temperature of 131°F for at least three days to destroy pathogens and render weeds inviable.

Some people want a lot of compost quickly and work to set up an ideal habitat for hot composting. Others aim to approximate the decomposition that takes place on the forest floor—cool, moist, and unhurried. It's the "make a nice pile and leave it alone" approach. Many so-called cold, or passive, piles never heat up significantly at all and rot nicely anyway. The end result is the same. In time, the decomposers will have broken down the organic matter into dark, humus-rich compost.

Inoculating Soil

There's a tendency to think of soil as dirt—inert, dull, lifeless. But in reality, it is a tremendously complex biological substance. A teaspoon can contain billions of microorganisms, representing thousands of species. Soil organisms provide a host of vital services for plants, including aiding in nutrient uptake, aerating the soil through burrowing and other activities, suppressing soil-borne diseases, and releasing nutrients into the soil through the decomposition of organic matter. One of the best ways to ensure the health of these organisms in your garden soil is to add compost.

Like the bacteria, fungi, and other creatures of the compost pile, most soil organisms need air, moisture, and organic matter to survive. By adding compost to your garden, you not only ensure that your beneficial soil microbes and bugs are getting a square meal, you also improve the habitat in which they live. It improves soil structure and thus the air and water resources for the organisms in the soil ecosystem. Furthermore, by adding compost, you're also inoculating your soil with billions more beneficial organisms, increasing the diversity of the soil. And a complex, living soil is a healthier, more stable soil in which no one organism is likely to erupt unchecked.

Decomposition is a spontaneous natural process, but if we understand it, we can nudge it in directions that suit us. Ask ten good gardeners the best way to compost, and you'll get ten different answers, but in each case the needs of the decomposers are looked after, and in each case the care is rewarded with rich, living soil.

Basic Ingredients and Techniques

Joseph Keyser

Now that you have a picture of the rich ecology involved in creating compost, it's time to learn how to nurture a productive community of decomposers in your own compost system. These organisms thrive under specific conditions, which you can very easily control. The balance of air, moisture, temperature, and ingredients (in particular those that are carbon rich and nitrogen rich) that you create will determine how vigorous your decomposers are and how fast and successfully they will complete their work. A hot, healthy pile can turn kitchen scraps and yard trimmings into compost in quick order—but maintaining a hot pile can be a lot of work. As you're learning more about composting techniques, think about which approach will work best for you given the particulars of your garden site, the time you are willing to put into maintaining your system, and the type and volume of material you are looking to compost.

Compostable Materials

Most residential composters use whatever compostable material they produce in their gardens and homes. Yard trimmings—leaves, grass, weeds, and prunings—make up the major share of compost ingredients, but kitchen scraps and household materials can also play a significant role. Here's what you need to know about some common organic materials that are appropriate for small-scale home composting.

Leaves Leaves are the carbon-rich basis of most piles in temperate areas and are generally the easiest material to manage. They can be composted whole, shredded by a lawn mower with a bagging attachment, or chopped up with a power shredder. As with all compostable materials, reducing particle size will accelerate the decomposition process. When you add a large volume of leaves to a pile or bin, moisten the pile as you go, using a hose with a spray attachment. It's almost impossible to add water to a leaf pile after the fact—it just sheds off the top.

Leaves composted all by themselves can become a humus-rich leaf mold in about one year if the pile is turned several times per season. The process can be hastened by incorporating nitrogen-rich materials like grass clippings and weeds, which will result in a finer, loamlike compost.

Get your compost pile off to a good start with some basic know-how and an appropriate mix of compostable materials.

It's important to know what to add to your pile, and it's just as important to know what to leave out. Don't let anyone add meat, dairy, or non-compostable trash to your bin.

Grass Clippings from the lawn are the second most widely composted yard material. They're full of nitrogen and can speed up the decomposition of carbonaceous materials such as leaves, straw, or chipped brush. Most savvy gardeners know that healthy lawns thrive when clippings are left on the lawn after mowing. However, if your grass has grown taller than four inches, it might be beneficial to remove heavy clumps of clippings and add them to the compost pile. You can also use grass clippings to jump-start a sluggish pile.

Grass should never be composted by itself—in fact, most odor complaints about compost piles result from those made up of clippings alone. Grass is more than 90 percent water, and the thin blades rapidly clump together, forming slimy, anaerobic masses that give off a strong ammonia odor. Use a garden fork to thoroughly mix grass into dry or higher-carbon materials.

Food Scraps Spoiled vegetables, fruits, and kitchen scraps provide a rich source of nitrogen. Coffee grounds contain as much nitrogen as grass clippings. Tea leaves and tea bags, corn husks and cobs, fruit rinds, vegetable trimmings and peels, and eggshells are all prime candidates for the pile. Breads and grains may be added as long as they aren't oily or mixed with any non-compostable ingredients. But be sure to avoid adding meat or dairy products—they have a dense, high-protein composition that is likely to attract anaerobic bacteria and create sulfide gases and odors of putrefaction. Various undesirable insects would also be more likely to breed on the pile, leaving behind larvae (maggots). Meat and dairy scraps will also attract larger, four-legged visitors like rodents and raccoons.

Bury all food items, including spoiled fruits taken directly from the garden, at least one foot into the compost pile. If you simply drop scraps onto the top, even in an enclosed bin, you're guaranteed to attract fruit flies, gnats, houseflies, and larger pests. In urban areas or communities with rodent problems, a completely enclosed unit, such as a lidded metal trash can with small holes, a bin lined with hardware cloth, or even an indoor worm bin, is recommended.

Woody Materials Hedge trimmings, small twigs and branches, stalks, wood chips (both old and new), pinecones, large seedpods, and other woody matter are extremely high in carbon and can help aerate a pile that contains a high proportion of food scraps. However, they will take longer to decompose than leaves. You can speed up their decomposition by chipping them, or at least cutting them up with shears or pruners. Avoid adding anything longer than your hand or thicker than your thumb. Larger materials will linger for years and make turning the pile more difficult.

Herbaceous Trimmings and Weeds In addition to materials from vegetable patches and lawns, ornamental grasses, vines, deadheaded flowers, spent annuals, perennial prunings, and most other herbaceous material in the garden can be added to the pile. As with woody trimmings, chop them up as much as possible first.

Kitchen scraps like fruit and vegetable peels are a key "green." Storing them in the freezer until it's time to add them to the pile will keep them from getting stinky in your kitchen.

Common herbaceous garden weeds are like lawn grasses—loaded with moisture and nitrogen—so they should be well mixed into the pile. Avoid adding those that have set seed or have vigorous rhizomes, especially invasive species like morning glory or Japanese knotweed. Unless, that is, you practice the hot composting method (see below), which can kill the whole weed, including its seeds. Most folks, however, practice the more passive cold method, which doesn't destroy viable seeds and may allow some weeds to use the pile as a launch pad to other inviting areas in your garden. If you'd rather not take your chances, you can use solarization to ensure that weed clippings won't cause any problems. Simply place the offending plants outside in a black plastic bag for a couple of months and let the sun turn them to mush before you work them into the pile.

Household Materials Compostable materials from around the house are usually carbon rich, including newspaper (most should be recycled, but small amounts can provide a carbon boost), corrugated and uncoated cardboard that is too soiled or wet for the recycling bin (the rest should be recycled), paper towels, dried flowers, wood or fireplace ash (never charcoal or coal ash), and untreated sawdust. Cardboard and newspaper should be ripped into strips and moistened, preferably by soaking in a bucket of water.

Agricultural Manures Animal manures are a wonderful source of nitrogen and other nutrients, especially for gardeners without access to grass clippings. Poultry

Fallen leaves are an important source of carbon. Collect them in autumn and keep some on hand for warmer months when "browns" are hard to come by.

What Not to Add

Good hygiene is as important for keeping the compost pile healthy as it is for your garden overall. Here's what to leave out.

Diseased plant materials Viruses and other pathogens aren't always destroyed in the composting process.

Pesticide-treated plants, including grass clippings Avoid especially if the finished product is to be used in a vegetable garden.

Pressure-treated wood scraps and sawdust Copper, cyanide, and arsenic may be present.

Poison sumac, poison ivy, and other irritating plants Toxic plant oils don't easily break down. Nettles and thorny twigs will decompose eventually, but beware of handling unfinished compost.

Food scraps containing oils, meats, or dairy products Fats in spreads and baked goods made with shortening will inhibit decomposition, and ingredients like sugar can attract pests. Meat and dairy scraps will also draw pests, create odors, and take a long time to break down.

Fecal waste of dogs, cats, or other carnivorous pets These manures may contain long-lived pathogens that persist in the garden.

Long-lasting organic materials Unless chipped into small pieces first, waxy leaves of magnolias and hollies, pinecones, sweet gum pods, and other materials that break down slowly are best left out of the pile.

manure is a concentrated source of nitrogen, although the odor is difficult to work around. Cow manure is one of the most valuable additions, although horse manure may be more readily available from stables, even in most urban areas. Keep in mind, though, that all manure may contain human pathogens. If you plan to use your compost on any edible plants, make sure that at least one year has passed between the time you add manure to your pile and the time you harvest.

Browns and Greens

All organic matter contains both carbon and nitrogen in varying quantities. To make good compost, you should feed your compost pile a balanced mix of carbon-rich (generally brown, dry) and nitrogen-rich (generally green, wet) material, so the resulting carbon-to-nitrogen (C:N) ratio comes to roughly 30:1. The strains of bacteria that are primarily responsible for decomposition are most successful when they ingest material at this ratio, using the carbon compounds for energy and growth and the nitrogen to synthesize proteins and genetic material.

In general, if you combine roughly equal parts browns and greens by volume, you'll get pretty close to the desired 30:1 ratio. Most deciduous leaves have a

Browns and Greens

Browns (carbon rich, dry)

- **Fallen leaves**
- **Wood chips**
- **Sawdust** Make sure it's not from pressure-treated wood.
- **Spent plants and potting soil** Avoid adding material from diseased or invasive plants.
- **Straw or hay** Avoid hay seeds; they may survive the composting process.
- **Pinecones and pine needles**
- **Twigs** Chop any that are thicker than your thumb into smaller pieces.
- **Newspaper** Not recommended in large amounts, a few sheets torn into strips can be added if you need a boost of carbon.
- **Eggshells** These are an excellent source of calcium.
- **Breads, grains, and beans** Bury under at least one foot of material to avoid attracting animal pests.
- **Corncobs** Chop into small pieces for faster breakdown.
- **Wood ashes** Add sparingly; never add ash from charcoal briquettes.
- **Paper towels and plates**
- **Corrugated or unwaxed cardboard** Composting is a good option for any cardboard that is too wet or soiled for recycling.

Greens (nitrogen rich, wet)

- **Kitchen scraps,** including fruit and vegetable peels and cores. Chop tough peels or large scraps.
- **Coffee grounds and tea bags** Filters and paper tags are okay too.
- **Fresh leaves and plants**
- **Weeds** Add before they set seed; omit pernicious plants like bindweed and quackgrass.
- **Spent cut flowers**
- **Freshly pruned trimmings** Chop woody ones into pieces.
- **Grass clippings** Mix thoroughly with other ingredients to avoid creating anaerobic conditions.
- **Seaweed** Add only small amounts to avoid high levels of salts.
- **Aquarium water** Use freshwater only; contains algae.
- **Manure and bedding** from farm animals and small pets like hamsters and rabbits. Avoid cat or dog litter.
- **Brewery waste** Spent grain from home-brewing kits is also good.
- **Feathers, fur, hair**

Perforated PVC pipes can be placed in your bin to help aerate it passively, a practice that is especially important for hot piles, which need plenty of oxygen to thrive.

C:N ratio between 50:1 and 70:1, while grass clippings, manures, and food scraps have a ratio between 10:1 and 20:1; woody materials can have a C:N ratio as high as 500:1. Too much nitrogen in a pile results in the formation of ammonia gas; too much carbon and the composting process will stall. A mix of different ingredients gives you a more favorable balance of carbon and nitrogen and a faster, harder-working compost pile. Diversifying your ingredients also leads to a greater diversity of decomposer organisms in your pile and results in a better-quality, more nutrient-rich compost.

Figuring out the ideal mix of materials usually requires some trial and error. The availability of greens and browns in your yard might vary throughout the year. Try collecting different types of materials as they become seasonably available. For example, in autumn and winter, gather fallen leaves and save them in a separate container to use when you need to balance a large volume of grass and other green plant matter in the spring and summer.

Moisture and Air

The microbes and other organisms that decompose the yard and kitchen waste in your compost pile also need a balanced supply of moisture and air in order to thrive. Promote good air circulation by mixing the compost regularly and thoroughly with a garden fork or other aeration tool (see "Bins and Other Equipment,"

Easy Composting Options for Yard Trimmings

All of the following materials can be added to your compost pile or returned to the soil more directly through one of these methods.

Grass

- Leave it on the lawn. When mowing, cut off no more than a third of the blades' height at a time using a regular or mulching mower.

- Use as mulch. Apply one inch deep on annual beds.

Leaves

- Chop them up with a regular or mulching mower and leave them on the lawn. This works for all but the heaviest leaf fall.

- Use as mulch for perennial beds, shrubs, or trees. Apply a one- to three-inch-thick layer, either whole or shredded with a mower or chipper/shredder.

- Sheet, trench, or pit compost. Bury or till under soil. (See page 43.)

Woody prunings, dead plants, and holiday greens

- Use as mulch. Chop or shred first, or use larger pieces for an informal look.

page 46)—shifting the inner material to the outside as often as every three to seven days. Mixing also helps distribute moisture equally throughout the bin. You may need to add water from time to time to maintain the proper moisture level. The compost should feel damp to the touch but not dripping wet—as moist as a wrung-out sponge is good rule of thumb. Remember: The drier the pile, the longer it will take to compost.

Temperature

Every compost pile will move through temperature fluctuations as the various populations of microbial decomposers go to work, but you may wish to control your pile's heat buildup for particular reasons. If you have a large volume of material to compost and are willing to devote some time toward maintaining it regularly, you can build a hot, fast-working pile in which heat-loving bacteria quickly break down the organics. If you'd rather be planting than composting, consider a slower, more passive, cold composting approach.

Fast, or Hot, Composting Hot piles are best suited for processing large quantities of greens and browns in roughly equal amounts. To help the smaller decomposers get right to work, ingredients should be chopped into fine pieces—the finer they are, the faster they break down. A hot pile needs to be at least three feet to a side (one cubic yard) in order to maintain the heat and moisture required to foster thermophilic decomposers. Any pile, regardless of size, can be kept warmer by insulating it with hay bales. Using such insulators is also an effective way of trapping compost heat in cold weather and extending the activity of compost microbes into the winter season.

A hot pile must be turned or aerated every three to seven days (whenever its temperature drops, indicating a slowdown in decomposition activity, or when the temperature rises above 150°). If you don't have time to turn your compost this frequently, you can help aerate it passively by placing perforated PVC pipes in your pile. A hot compost pile typically takes about six weeks to three months to decompose. You can "batch compost" by actively managing one pile while collecting material for the next. Set aside leaves and other browns in a holding bin or freestanding heap and store food scraps in the freezer or refrigerator until you have enough of both to start the next batch.

The hot-composting process will usually kill off weed seeds, fly larvae, and disease pathogens in the pile and give you a more uniform, decomposed product. On the downside, hot compost contains less nitrogen and is less hospitable to disease-suppressing organisms such as fungi and nematodes compared with cold compost.

Slow, or Cold, Composting All organic matter will rot, no matter what you do or don't do to it. For slow and easy compost, there's no need to assemble all your ingredients before you start—just add materials as they become available. When the pile gets to be about four to five feet wide by three feet high, leave it alone,

Hot piles reach temperatures above 130°F, high enough to kill most weed seeds and pathogens. They also produce finished compost quickly but take some effort to maintain.

Hot or Cold? What Works Best for You?

Speedy and Steamy

- Materials are added all at once
- Requires large volume of equal parts browns and greens
- Material must be chopped into small pieces
- Needs regular maintenance
- Finished compost: 6 weeks to 3 months

Slow and Steady

- Materials can be added over time
- Allows various materials to be added as they become available
- Material can be added in larger pieces
- Mostly maintains itself
- Finished compost: 6 months to years

or give it the occasional stir. Even though their temperatures might climb above 100°F, slow piles are often referred to as cold, since the temperature peak isn't as high and doesn't last as long as in a fast pile. You can usually harvest finished compost in six months to two years.

The major advantage of cold composting is that it's low maintenance: You don't have to be as careful about balancing your materials or mixing and watering. Cold composting also conserves more nitrogen and fosters greater amounts of beneficial fungi in the finished product compared with hot composting. On the downside, cold piles are exposed to the elements for long periods and so are more susceptible to nutrient leaching. And because temperatures don't soar, weed seeds and pathogens will likely survive the cold-composting process. Also, the finished product is not as uniform as hot-composted material and may contain undecomposed matter that requires screening.

Compostable Plastic in Your Bin?

Niall Dunne

Recently, manufacturers have been offering "compostable plastic" items like dinnerware, waste bags, and packaging as eco-friendly alternatives to traditional plastic. Most are made of renewable, plant-based material or "bioplastic." Sounds like a win-win situation.

Unfortunately, it's not that simple. Many of these products aren't suitable for backyard composting systems. If you read the fine print, you'll see a lot of them, especially the harder plastic items like utensils, are meant to be composted at high temperatures only achievable in commercial sites, and not all collection sites accept them. To make matters worse, these items are usually not recyclable, but many get wrongly sorted into the recycling bin, and they can gum up the works at the recycling facility. Others end up in landfills, where they break down under anaerobic conditions, releasing methane, a potent greenhouse gas.

Of course it's always best to choose reusable products over any kind of disposable ones, be they compostable or recyclable. Still, even the most environmentally conscious among us need to use a disposable plate or bag on occasion, so it's good news that manufacturers are responding to the demand for greener products. With any luck, more home-compostable products will be developed, and more collection sites will accept compostable plastic. In the meantime, a Belgian organization has developed the OK Compost Home benchmark for identifying products that break down in a home system. (See their test results at okcompost.be/en.)

If you're game for experimenting, you can always run a few trials in your own pile and see what kind of results you get. It will help to have a big, hot pile and to keep your expectations low. "We tested out a variety of these items, and not that many

actually broke down in our piles—and they're much hotter and bigger than what most people have at home," says Jenny Blackwell, project manager for the NYC Compost Project in Brooklyn.

Softer, thinner items like plates, cups, or bags—anything that can be ripped or shredded—stand a better chance of breaking down in a reasonable amount of time than harder items like utensils. Start with a small quantity, rip or shred them up, and see how well they break down after six months or so. If they seem to be decomposing nicely, you can gradually increase the proportion to suit your needs.

Composting in Practice
Elizabeth Peters

There are all sorts of ways to compost, from going it alone in your apartment to sharing a bin system with your neighbors to joining a neighborhood or city greening project. There are even programs that certify master composters—trained volunteers who share their expertise with the community—including one based at Brooklyn Botanic Garden (bbg.org/composting).

Ask your friends about composting, and you may be surprised to learn you already know some experienced compost practitioners who could give you plenty of tips. Or check with your local community gardens, public gardens, and other environmental programs to find classes, demonstration sites, and established systems. Avid composters are a community-minded bunch, and you'll likely find that they are more than happy to share war stories and practical advice. Seeing composting in action can reassure you that it's not hard, and maybe more important, that done right, it's not smelly. Problems will always arise, but for the most part small adjustments (as described in the coming chapters) will solve them.

The snapshots of real-life projects on the next few pages demonstrate some different ways to compost. Before you get started, a few general words of advice:

Find a local program to join or visit. Contributing to an established compost program requires a smaller commitment than starting your own bin and is a great way to begin. Most programs offer orientations or training. Once you know the basics, you'll have a better idea of what will work best for you.

Composting doesn't have to be perfect. Remember, decomposition happens just fine on its own. If you sometimes have to neglect your system, it usually just means the process will take a bit longer. When you're ready to renew your efforts, things will speed right back up.

Get the whole family involved. Most kids love the "ick" factor of decomposition. Involve them in the chores of composting: separating waste, bringing material to the bin or drop-off site, and using finished compost to nurture new plants. It's a great way to inspire young naturalists.

INDOORS

System Worm Factory 360 indoor/outdoor composter

What's Happening Worm composting is just the thing for this apartment dweller who travels a lot. He was motivated to try it out a few years ago when he joined a CSA and suddenly had a large quantity of vegetable scraps. Now he chops them up and buries them in his worm bin, which he keeps under his kitchen table. The worms quietly and odorlessly turn the scraps into compost, which he gives to friends or surreptitiously adds to neighborhood gardens that look as if they could use a boost. Every few weeks he'll add torn-up paper as bedding material, which he keeps moist; a layer of dry paper on top keeps out flies (the tower itself is well sealed). The worms can survive for up to two weeks without attention, which means he doesn't have to worry about them while traveling. Plus, his regular trash goes out much less frequently because there is nothing smelly collecting in it.

Lessons Learned Worm composting is actually very easy to do! You just have to be willing to get your hands dirty.

BACKYARD

System Garden Gourmet recycled-plastic bin

What's Happening This Brooklynite composts using a plastic bin that a previous tenant left in his building's shared yard. He saves food scraps in a kitchen pail, then adds them to the bin along with a handful of dead leaves stockpiled from fall. About once a week he removes the cover and turns the compost with a crank; he's never had to water it because the covered bin conserves just the right amount of moisture. In spring and midsummer he removes a batch of compost, screens out the larger pieces, then sets it aside to mellow until he's ready to use it in the small yard.

Lessons Learned Pests were never a concern until a nearby construction project drove rats out of their nests. The bin was successfully fortified against them with an interior layer of chicken wire and a stack of bricks around the base. Although he personally prefers the open-bin composting systems he's used in the past, he thinks a covered composter is a great option for space-challenged city dwellers who need to allay any fears their neighbors have about pests and odors.

ROOFTOP

System Homemade bins: three modified trash cans, homemade tumbler, two pickle barrels, storage for browns and finished compost

What's Happening The 16 residents of this Brooklyn apartment building began composting their organic waste in 2008, when they persuaded the building's owner to provide rooftop access for their setup. Fresh scraps along with brown material go into a designated bin; once full, the bin is left to progress through the decomposition stages. Finished compost is moved to a tumbler to cure, then sifted and used to improve the building's yard. It's a fairly low-intensity setup: Every few months a pair of residents spend a few hours turning and tending the bins, but in between they are pretty much left alone. Compost is ready in about six months.

Lessons Learned A big factor in this system's success was making it easy for all residents to use correctly. Clear signage, written instructions, and browns kept readily at hand helps, as does one-on-one training. The composters are careful to take care of the roof and have won over the originally skeptical building manager.

COMMUNITY GARDEN

System Three wooden bins; three Garden Gourmet bins; two Earth Machine bins; two circular plastic curing corrals; a repurposed dryer drum to hold browns

What's Happening 6/15 Green, a community garden in Brooklyn, offers compost memberships to about 50 people who volunteer their time to maintain the system, which processes waste from the garden and local businesses as well as kitchen scraps dropped off by area residents. Each person who contributes is responsible for mixing in his or her scraps; everyone learns about composting at orientation sessions and through literature offered on-site and on the garden's website (615green.org). Finished compost is used in the garden and by participants. The program, started in 1994, is operating at capacity; rather than expanding it, organizers are focusing on sharing information and offering on-site training to other community groups.

Lessons Learned Match the system you establish to a realistic assessment of the amount of participation/labor/resources you'll have. After you see what's working, you can grow your program little by little.

MUNICIPAL SITE

System Multiple windrows (long rows of compost) with forced-air ventilation, sited on property owned by the New York City Department of Parks and Recreation

What's Happening BIG!Compost (bignyc.org/compost) is one of several community greening programs that coordinate the processing of residential food scraps in partnership with the NYC Department of Sanitation (see page 103). Scraps collected at farmers' markets and other drop-off sites are brought to local composting facilities where volunteers mix them with dried leaves, wood chips, and finished compost, then construct five-foot-tall windrows. To foster aerobic decomposition, every half hour, air is pumped for 30 seconds through PVC pipes laid in the base of the piles. After about two months, the decomposed matter is moved off the pipes to cure for an additional month. Mature compost is then screened; larger bits are added to new piles, and the remainder is used to nourish urban green spaces.

Lessons Learned Just a year old, the program is really taking hold. Participants love watching the full circle of waste become a resource for public beautification.

Establishing and Maintaining a System

Patricia Jasaitis

Once you've considered the amount and types of compostables you have and decided which method you'd like to try, you'll need to set up an appropriate system to handle it all and learn how to manage it. No matter what approach you take, you'll do a lot of learning on the job. Still, putting some forethought into how the process will work will make operations proceed much more smoothly.

Site Considerations

When choosing a location for your system, look for a level, easily accessible spot, near a water source if possible. As a good-neighbor policy, don't site your pile right on your property line or next to the neighbor's patio or window. You'll also want to place your system at least a foot away from any wooden structures—the fungi in your pile won't discriminate between your fence and the twigs and trimmings that you want to decompose. Likewise, don't place bins or piles against a tree trunk—this could create a suitable environment for pests or diseases to attack the tree, and it may impede airflow to your tree's root system. If rodents are a concern, also avoid placing your system against a wall, since rats and mice like to travel along narrow corridors. Instead, leave at least a foot of open space. If you grow vegetables, consider setting your pile among the planting beds, so nutrients that leach out of the bottom can enrich the soil and feed your plants. Most systems do equally well in sun or shade, but gardeners in hot, dry climates should choose shade, where their compost is less likely to dry out, and those in colder ones might want to choose a sunny spot so ingredients are less likely to freeze in winter.

Bins and Freestanding Heaps

For gardeners in rural and suburban areas, a freestanding pile on bare ground may work well. For many urban gardeners, however, composting in a bin or other container—one that's resistant to rodents—is usually essential. Compost bins come in a wide spectrum of designs (see "Bins and Other Equipment," page 46) and offer other benefits besides the ability to keep out pests. Bins contain your compost in a com-

Choose the right compost system for your situation and manage it well, and you will be rewarded with good-quality finished compost.

pact area and keep your garden tidy; they concentrate materials in a smaller volume, retaining moisture and warmth, which encourages biological activity; and they allow more control over the composting process, such as the ability to keep rainfall out. Some also allow you to access more mature compost from the bottom of the pile via a drawer or removable slats.

Choose a bin or system that will accommodate the volume of material you generate. Many composters maintain a system of two or more bins. Not only does this allow you to accommodate a high volume of material, it also helps make the best use of compost at different stages. You can designate one bin for "receiving" and the other for "curing." If you are cold composting, you can, say, fill one bin over the course of a year and start a second bin while the first bin is maturing. Then you can wait and harvest finished compost from the older bin when it's ready with minimal turning and management. A multi-bin system is also handy for hot composting; use one bin for cooking, the other for storing browns in preparation for your next hot pile.

Composters in wet climates may need to cover their bins so rain or snow doesn't waterlog the pile or allow nutrients to leach away. If you live in a temperate climate, your bin will benefit from being open to the elements. Periodic rainfall can provide most of the moisture needed for optimal composting; making a funnel-shaped depression in the top of the pile will help capture it. Cover the bin in cold months,

The material in your pile should be about as moist as a wrung-out sponge. If it is too dry, adding some water will encourage decomposition and deter ants and bees.

A community garden usually requires a multi-bin system, not only to hold a high volume of compost but also to allow finished batches to be used while newer batches "cook."

though, when biological activity slows and additional moisture may only leach away nutrients. Freestanding piles or heaps in the country may also need some protection from wildlife or pets. This can be accomplished using screens or fencing.

Managing the System

Before you begin adding browns and greens to your bin or heap, lay down a layer of wood chips or other coarse organic matter at the bottom to increase aeration and allow excess water to drain. As you add material to the pile, keep in mind the goal of balancing greens and browns. Avoid layering material "lasagna" style (unless you are intentionally sheet composting; see page 43.) Layering without mixing can keep oxygen from permeating the compost, fostering anaerobic activity that may promote bad odors. Instead, bury new material, especially kitchen scraps, well inside the compost pile and cover it with brown material like dried leaves. In a couple of days, mix it up again. Monitor the system's moisture level and temperature, and be alert for the need for aeration. See "Troubleshooting Tips" pages 41–42 for additional maintenance advice.

If you are composting in a heap, be sure that your pile doesn't get too tall: A pile over five feet high will be hard to manage. The organic matter will become severely compacted and the circulation of oxygen in the pile will be reduced or cut off, resulting in anaerobic conditions and sluggish breakdown. In wet climates, you can

Proper aeration is key to maintaining a good pile. It will encourage aerobic decomposition, prevent odors, and help maintain optimal temperatures.

minimize the risk of waterlogging by spreading straw on top of your pile; it will help shed water without affecting aeration.

The composting process will eventually reduce the volume of the original material in your pile by about half. The time it takes to finish breaking down will depend on a variety of factors: the type of original material, its texture (smaller, finer stuff composts faster), the volume of your pile, the amount of aeration you provide, and so forth. For most backyard composting, which usually ends up being a hybrid of cold and hot methods, it may take 6 to 12 months for a pile to finish. If you monitor the pile's temperature, you'll know you're getting close when the temperature drops after the thermophilic phase.

Finished compost is dark and crumbly, resembling very fertile topsoil, with a pleasant earthy smell. A quick test to see if your compost is finished: Place some compost in a plastic bag and seal it. Wait a few days, open the bag, and take a whiff. If doesn't smell bad, your compost is done. If it smells rotten, put it back—it's not finished. Or, you can perform a cress test (see page 78).

When harvesting from a cold pile, you may have to dig down toward the bottom to find the finished stuff. Large undecomposed pieces of organic matter can be sifted out with a wire mesh screen and either discarded or returned to the pile. Stubborn materials, such as corncobs, may make many trips through the compost pile before

Troubleshooting Tips

PROBLEM	CAUSE	SOLUTION
Bad odor (like spoiled food)	Uncovered or inappropriate food scraps	Remove and discard any improper materials (meats, dairy, etc.); bury food scraps under a foot or more of browns in the pile.
Bad odor (like rotten eggs, pond scum, swamp gas)	Anaerobic conditions; too much moisture	Turn materials; mix in browns—dry leaves, straw, or wood chips—to absorb moisture and let in air. Check base of pile for proper drainage. Leave lid off to improve airflow.
Bad odor (strong ammonia, moldy hay)	Too much nitrogen-rich, green material (such as grass)	Mix in browns (dry or high-carbon materials). Remove some greens, spread them out to dry for a few days, then mix back into pile.
Pile not breaking down	Insufficient nitrogen, moisture, or aeration	To increase nitrogen, add grass, manure, kitchen scraps, coffee grounds, and other "fresh" materials. To increase moisture, add water while turning pile until it feels like a damp sponge throughout. For more aeration, turn and mix materials more often. Also check the integrity of the pile's base and replace if necessary. Consider switching to a bin or system with better aeration, for instance, one to which aeration tubes have been added.
Pile heats up, then stops	Poor aeration; insufficient nitrogen	Turn materials regularly. It might also be necessary to periodically add an additional nitrogen source, such as fresh-cut grass clippings.

PROBLEM	CAUSE	SOLUTION
Pile too cold, even in warm months	Pile too small	Binned piles require about nine cubic feet to work efficiently. Add more materials if possible, or use a smaller bin to concentrate the pile's volume.
Pile too cold in winter	Inadequate insulation	To keep the environment congenial for your mesophilic and thermophilic decomposers, insulate with Styrofoam or hay bales to hold heat in.
Pile too hot (over 150°F)	Pile too large; improper aeration	Reduce the pile's size, add water, or turn materials more frequently to release heat and redistribute organic matter.
Insect pests	Pile inadequately mixed or too dry; contaminated mulch or other woody material added	Make sure food scraps are properly buried, and turn the outer layer of materials into the pile's core. Hot piles will destroy or repel most pests, such as grubs, maggots, and other larvae. Moist piles deter bees and wasps, so add more water if necessary. Wood chips and material taken from rotted wood piles or municipal mulch piles may contain termites or carpenter ants, so check all materials carefully before introducing them to pile.
Animal pests	Food scraps left exposed or inadequate bin for location	Bury food well under other materials, keep the pile moist, and turn frequently to disturb nests. For persistent problems, especially with rodents, stop adding food scraps, use an enclosed bin, or change the bin design to restrict access. To deter burrowers, line the bin with hardware cloth or screen, extending it six to eight inches below the ground. A secure lid will discourage opossums, raccoons, and birds.

Composting often involves some sleuthing. A bad odor could mean your pile needs more air, or it might be that an inappropriate item, like a meat or poultry scrap, was added.

they eventually break down. For instructions on how to spread compost or incorporate it into your soil, see "Using Compost in the Garden," page 76.

Alternatives to the Pile

If you have a relatively large garden with minimal concerns about rodents or other pests, you might consider composting on the spot in a pit or trench or try sheet composting.

Pit and Trench Composting Pit composting involves burying chopped food scraps or garden trimmings directly in 8- to 12-inch-deep holes around the garden. Trench composting is similar, but the holes are larger (12 to 18 inches deep, a yard wide, and as long as needed) and they should be filled with a mix of greens and browns before being covered with soil. Once a pit or trench is buried, it's best not to uncover it for a while—organic matter decomposes anaerobically underground and will smell sour until it is finished. In six months to a year, the process should be complete and you can plant your pit or trench.

Sheet Composting Spread a batch of leaves, manure, or other organics onto the soil and mix it in with a fork or rototiller; this is sheet composting. You can apply a layer up to eight inches thick. Allow the materials to decay for a few months before planting. See page 98 for detailed instructions for using this method in raised beds.

Debunking Composting Myths

Joseph Keyser

Let's keep composting simple and inexpensive by putting some common misconceptions to rest.

Composting is smelly.

Not so. A properly built and managed compost pile should smell earthy, like the forest floor. Odors result primarily from mistakes: trying to compost grass clippings by themselves, adding too many food scraps (or the wrong types of food), or allowing either too much water or too little air, both of which will lead to anaerobic conditions.

Your pile is sure to harbor rats.

Untrue. Though it is important to choose the right bin and manage your compost properly, especially in urban areas, rodent infestations are preventable. Trash containers, birdfeeders, outdoor pet-food bowls, and pet feces are all far more likely to attract unwanted critters than a well-managed compost bin. Simple measures like burying food scraps under a layer of neutral material will go a long way toward deterring scavengers. Other rodent-proofing strategies—like using an enclosed bin or forgoing food scraps—can also be employed for persistent problems. (See "Composting in the City," page 92.)

You must obsessively calculate carbon-to-nitrogen ratios.

Books, articles, and brochures sometimes fixate on carbon-to-nitrogen ratios, but in truth, there's a pretty wide range of conditions under which a pile can thrive. Tinkering with the ratio can be fun for hobbyists, but most gardeners need only remember that all organic materials will compost in a timely manner given some prudent attention.

You can create good compost in two weeks.
Misguided claims and gimmicky marketing abound for special tools and materials
that can drastically reduce decomposition time. But though producing compost
quickly has its benefits, no one should feel compelled to purchase elaborate
equipment to speed things up. And remember, even if material looks like compost
after just a few weeks, a month of curing is still recommended to allow the compost to
fully finish and reach an appropriate pH level.

You need to buy special bioactivators to provide the right microorganisms.
These bacteria-laden powders and liquids are the snake oil of composting. Though
they do contain "cultured" strains of bacteria and other additives, such special
inoculants are unnecessary. Studies estimate that there are millions to billions of
bacteria in a spoonful of garden soil. Every fallen leaf and blade of grass you add to
your pile is already covered with thousands of microorganisms—more than enough
to do the job. If you want to jump-start things, adding a handful of active compost
will suffice.

Adding yeast, worms, or soft drinks will give your pile a boost.
Many strategies touted for improving compost performance are unnecessary,
unsubstantiated, and flat-out silly. Some practitioners, for instance, suggest
pouring cola into the pile to increase beneficial biological activity. In reality, all it
will do is draw yellow jackets and ants. Adding yeast, another common suggestion,
is expensive and useless. The idea of adding worms to outdoor piles has also
emerged due to confusion with indoor vermicomposting, but earthworms need not
be purchased or brought in: Just build your pile and they will come on their own. Red
wiggler worms, the species used for vermicomposting, will usually not survive in an
outdoor pile in colder climates.

Adding commercial fertilizer will increase nitrogen content in the pile.
Synthetically derived fertilizers contain high levels of salts and other compounds,
which are harmful to worms and microorganisms. They may actually impair the
nitrogen-fixing ability of the bacteria and short-circuit the nitrogen cycle in a compost
pile. If you need to increase nitrogen—maybe your pile has an overabundance of
carbon-rich leaves—try organic sources first, such as coffee grounds, grass clippings,
or agricultural manures.

Lime will help you reach the right pH level.
Gardeners with a high proportion of acid-rich compost materials might think adding
lime will help neutralize their pile's pH, but actually, ground limestone will turn your
compost ecosystem into an ammonia factory, with nitrogen rapidly lost as a noxious
gas. When compost is left alone, the volatilization of organic acids and incorporation
of ammonia into new microbial growth tends to even out pH regardless of the initial
composition of the pile. Compost almost always becomes nearly neutral (with a pH
between 6 and 8) by the time it is finished.

Bins and Other Equipment
Beth Hanson

If you're a casual, carefree sort, you can just toss your organics into a corner of the garden, and they'll slowly turn into rich compost without any intervention. But if you have the time and inclination to practice fast composting, you will need to outfit yourself with some of the tools of the trade. If you live in an urban area, you should buy—or construct—a bin to protect your compost pile from the attention of rodents and other scavengers. Below is a description of the composting arsenal; all of these items are available through a variety of online retailers and catalog companies (see page 104 for a list of sources), and many can be found in garden centers.

Compost Bins

The most widely available composting tool is the bin, which will neaten up your yard, speed the composting process by consolidating ingredients, and keep unwanted critters away from your pile. To decide what kind of bin is right for you, consider the amount and type of material you have to compost, your site, and your budget. Bins vary in price from about $25 for a simple wood-frame composter to as much as $500 for a high-end, steel-framed tumbler. A range of DIY and repurposing options exist too. Wooden pallets, plastic or wooden crates, or wine barrels can all be fashioned into useful bins. See page 54 for two wooden bin designs with complete instructions—a divided bin and a space-saving bench composter.

Whether you buy a bin or make your own, make sure the one you choose is easy to open and allows access for both adding raw materials and unloading finished compost. All bins should be vented in some way to allow air to circulate through the pile; look for one with a lid if you need to regulate moisture, depending on your climate and the ratio of materials you're composting. Many store-bought bins are made from plastic—sometimes recycled—and these tend to be lighter in weight and more durable than those made from other materials.

Wooden bins are a great-looking option but will gradually decay since microorganisms working on the compost will break down the wood too. Choose naturally rot-resistant wood such as cedar or hemlock to extend your bin's life span, or plan to replace rotted pieces periodically. You can also protect a wooden bin by treating

You can select from a wide variety of store-bought compost bins and accessories like collection pails. You can also build your own out of wood or other materials.

it with a nontoxic weatherproofing substance such as Thompson's WaterSeal or linseed oil, but avoid pressure-treated lumber; it may contain toxins that can leach into your compost. Metal models are another attractive option, but be aware that they will eventually rust out.

If rodents or raccoons are a potential problem, make sure that your bin is fully enclosed and rodent resistant, with air vents no larger than a quarter inch to deter mice. Look for bins with rodent screens on the bottom or add your own screen cut from wire mesh or hardware cloth. Bury the screen vertically six to eight inches deep to discourage burrowers.

Here are some common compost containers:

Adjustable Mesh or Wire Bin

Pros Inexpensive, easy to access, adjustable
Cons Not rodent resistant
Best Uses Holding leaves until your main pile needs browns

One of the most basic and inexpensive bins you can buy consists of an open-ended cylinder of rugged plastic netting. The sides of the bin are adjustable, so the overall volume can be increased or decreased to suit the amount of organic materials available. This lightweight bin usually needs to be staked to the ground to keep it in place. A popular model is the Geobin Composting System (geobin123.com; $32), which has a maximum capacity of about 17 cubic feet. Simple DIY versions can also be created with chicken wire and wooden stakes. Since this type of bin is open and unprotected, it's not a good choice for composting kitchen scraps in urban areas.

Slatted Wooden Bin

Pros Nice looking, convenient
Cons Can be expensive; will eventually deteriorate; usually requires extra steps for rodent proofing
Best Uses Multichamber models for community gardens, small ones for backyards

A simple and handsome option—this is basically a wooden box in which the side slats are spaced apart for ventilation. Many versions feature doors or removable slats to make it easier to turn and remove the compost, and some designs include internal walls so they can hold two or three separate batches at once. Sizes of commercial models vary; some are open, and others come with lids. Many designs incorporate metal mesh or hardware cloth, which allows good airflow while keeping out rats and mice. (It's also possible to line a slatted bin with hardware cloth to fortify it against pests.)

Bins come in a wide array of homemade and store-bought designs, including (clockwise from top left) the Garden Gourmet, a slatted wooden bin, an adjustable mesh bin, a Gardener's Supply Company tumbler, a modified trash can, and the ComposTumbler.

A drum sifter can be made of mesh and bicycle wheel rims. This one was even hooked up to an exercise bike to make rotating easier.

Modified Trash Can

Pros Compact, secure, inexpensive, easy to create
Cons Limited capacity; easily mistaken for garbage can; difficult to harvest compost
Best Uses Small urban gardens, patios, rooftops

An easy way to make your own compost bin is to drill holes (a quarter inch or bigger) in the bottom, sides, and lid of an ordinary metal or plastic trash can. The holes allow for air circulation and drainage, the snug-fitting lid deters hungry animals, and you can easily turn your pile by turning the bin on its side and rolling it. Use a bungee cord to help secure the lid if needed. Behrens manufactures a three-cubic-foot steel can complete with ventilation holes (behrensmfg.com; $30). This compact container is a great choice for composters with limited space.

Bottom-Access Plastic Bin

Pros Convenient, compact, moderately priced
Cons Less attractive than wooden bins
Best Uses Backyards, apartment building courtyards, small school gardens

When harvesting compost from a cold pile, you need to remove it from the bottom, so some bin models are designed with a sliding drawer at the base to make it easy to access. The Soilsaver Classic Composter (triformis.com; $95) and Garden

Gourmet (gardengourmet.com; $76) are two popular examples. Both are compact (about 11 cubic feet), easy to fill, have lids to keep rodents and excess moisture out, provide good aeration, and are made from 100 percent recycled materials.

Tumbler

Pros Convenient, compact, rodent resistant
Cons Some models difficult to turn and access; often expensive
Best Uses Rooftops, urban backyards

Some bins can be rotated; these "tumblers" are designed to make turning the compost easier. The fully enclosed bins have the added advantage of being relatively tidy and pest resistant. They also hold in moisture, a plus for composting on rooftops, which tend to be hotter and drier than the ground. Common tumbler models are drum-shaped bins that spin on a base covered with little rollers, but there are also orb-shaped versions that you turn by rolling around the yard. Some work well and others don't. Be sure the composter you choose is convenient to load and unload and extremely easy to turn—wet compost is heavy.

Aerating Tools

An excellent way to get oxygen to the hardworking organisms in your compost pile is to turn it regularly with a pitchfork or garden fork. There are also tools that have been designed especially to aerate compost piles. When thrust into the pile, they create long air shafts and stir the contents around a bit; they also minimize your upper-body workout. These compost-ventilating tools are basically long plastic or metal rods with handles. Some have small paddles or wings that are closed against the shaft as you plunge it into the pile and are supposed to open up (they sometimes don't) as you pull it out, mixing the organics. A popular model is the Compost Crank, which works like a very long corkscrew (lotechproducts.com; $52). Expect to spend from $20 to $60 for a typical aerating tool.

Screens

If you plan to use your compost in potting soil or to top-dress the lawn—or for any other purpose that requires excluding large clumps, stones, or other debris—a screen (also called a sifter, sieve, or riddle) can be very helpful. Small commercial screens have rails that allow them to sit atop a cart or wheelbarrow. One model is a large tub on legs with a screen for its bottom. Multiple DIY versions exist too, like the drum sifter pictured on the previous page. (Instructables offers information on building a pared-down version; see page 104.) You can also make a small sieve by stretching a piece of quarter- or half-inch hardware cloth over a wooden frame and securing it to the sides with brads or industrial staples. Or consider adapting a storage basket for this purpose.

Shredders and Chippers

Small pieces of organic material decompose faster because they have more surface area than larger ones. To that end, a chipper or shredder can be a worthwhile investment. A small shredder can be had for $150; a heavy-duty commercial machine will run into the thousands. But if you're into making hot compost and have lots of large yard waste—tree branches, for example—or bags and bags of leaves that you'd like to compost quickly, it may be worth sharing one with your neighbors or investing in one for your local community garden.

Shredders are designed to break up leaves, twigs, and other light plant matter. Material is dropped into the shredder's chute and passes by a spinning drum which has blades attached to it. Chippers are similar but have blades that can cut larger branches and brush into small chunks. Combination shredder-chippers are also available. Wear protective goggles and earplugs when using this equipment and follow the manufacturer's instructions assiduously.

Shears

For smaller operations, your pruning shears or loppers can be a useful low-tech alternative to a chipper or shredder. Use them to chop up twigs or small branches into bits before adding them to your pile.

Household objects can sometimes be used as composting tools. This plastic basket makes a fine sifter since it has holes at the bottom.

Mulching Mowers

Mulching mowers and add-on kits for regular mowers chop grass into fine pieces. You can leave this shredded grass on the lawn, where it will break down into the soil, or gather it to throw onto the compost pile. Regular mowers can be used for mulch mowing too, if you keep the blades sharp and cut off only a third of the grass's height. You can also mow over leaves to turn them into mulch or compost ingredients. A walk-behind mulching mower can cost from around $150 to $700.

Forks and Shovels

Garden tools you probably have on hand for other purposes will also come in handy for your compost pile. A garden fork or pitchfork, for instance, can be used to turn or move your pile, and a scoop shovel can be used to access materials at the bottom.

Compost Collection Pails

You can collect compostable materials in just about any watertight container, preferably one with a lid. You can also purchase a pail designed especially for this purpose, including chic stainless-steel pails with tight-fitting lids and brightly colored plastic buckets with replaceable charcoal filters. Prices range from $15 to $60.

For kitchen scraps, consider a bin that will fit in your freezer, which will minimize odors and pest problems. (Alternately, you could freeze your scraps in extra-large ziplock bags, empty milk cartons, or plastic grocery bags.) Be sure to chop the scraps before you freeze them—that way you can throw your frozen organics straight onto the pile. Frozen material is also easier to transport without danger of leaks or odors, a boon for urban composters who bring their materials to a local community garden or composting program. Dry, brown materials can be kept near your pile in a covered trash bin or plastic garbage bag, so that when you add fresh green materials to the pile, you're always prepared to match its volume with an equal amount of carbon-rich browns.

Compost Thermometers

Stick your pitchfork into the center of your compost pile; if the tines are hot to the touch when you pull out the fork, your pile is cooking. If that doesn't tell you enough about the temperature inside your pile, you may want to invest in a compost thermometer. If you're hoping to do hot composting to kill weed seeds and pathogens, your pile needs to reach at least 131°F and remain at that temperature for 72 hours. With a thermometer, you can be sure you've gotten it right. Thermometers can also help identify problems with piles that are running too cold or too hot. They range from 12 inches to 48 inches long and cost between about $25 and $250.

Build Your Own Composter

Jon Pope

Here are plans for two wooden bins: a bench, which has some curved and angled pieces and requires some advanced carpentry skills (above), and a two-bin composter, which is easier to assemble since it has no curved or angled pieces. For either, construction will be easier if you have a friend help. Make your bin from a rot-resistant wood such as cedar. You can also use pine, which is cheaper, but you will need to replace parts as they decay. Many lumberyards sell lumber cut to size and will sell you the specific pieces you need if you provide the list. They will probably not cut the curves and angles, so you will need a jigsaw to cut those. Label your cut wood pieces with chalk or pencil to make assembly easier. You'll also need a drill to predrill screw holes to avoid splitting the wood where thin pieces join and near the edges of boards.

Two-Bin Composter

Cost $800 for cedar; $300 for pine
Time 5 hours
Skill level Intermediate

Tools and Supplies
Tape Measure
Pencil
Drill with driving attachment
Steel square
Tin snips

Wood
A 6 posts 3" × 3 ½" × 31 ½"
B 10 front slats ¾" × 5 ½" × 35 ¾"
C 10 side slats ¾" × 5 ½" × 42"
D 5 back slats ¾" × 5 ½" × 82 ½"
E 5 divider wall slats ¾" × 5 ½" × 34 ¼"
F 1 cover piece ¾" × 3 ½" × 42"
G 1 cross-piece 1 ½" × 3 ½" × 84"
H 12 stops ¾" × 1 ¼" × 31 ½"
I 8 spacers ¾" × 1" × 2"
J 4 short panel supports 2" × 2" × 13"
K 4 long panel supports 2" × 2" × 18 ½"
L 2 nailers 1 ½" × 3 ½" × 8"
M 6 medium lid slats ¾" × 5 ½" × 41"
N 4 short lid slats ¾" × 5 ½" × 25 ½"

Hardware
6" heavy-duty hasp, galvanized finish
3" × 3" butt hinge
4 @ 1½" × 3" hinges
116 @ #10 2 ½" phillips-head or square-
  drive screws, galvanized or deck
36 @ 1 ½" galvanized or deck screws (for
  attaching stops)
12 @ #10 3" galvanized or deck screws
80 @ ⅝" #10 screws
80 @ 1" fender washers
16 @ 4" mending plates
36' x 3' quarter-inch hardware cloth

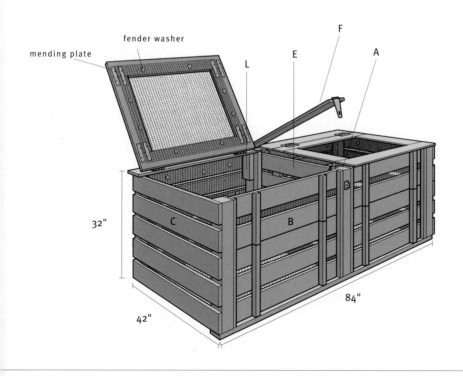

Build the back wall. Attach the five back slats (D) to two of the posts (A) with the 2 ½" screws (Figure 1). The edges of the top and bottom slats should be flush with the tops and bottoms of the posts, and the three middle slats should be spaced evenly between, leaving gaps of approximately one inch. The ends of the slats should also be flush with the outside of the posts. Use a square to make sure that the slats are square on the posts.

Build and attach the side walls. Attach two side slats (C) to one of the remaining posts (A) at the top and bottom so that they are flush with the tops and bottoms of the post. Stand the back wall upright, and attach the loose ends of the side slats to the back post. The side slats should be aligned with the top and bottom back slats (Figure 2). Then attach the middle side slats so that they are in alignment with the corresponding back slats. Repeat this step for the other side of your bin. You should now have a three-sided box.

Line the back of the bin with hardware cloth. Cut this material to fit using tin snips or some other heavy-duty shears. Make sure, if you are using multiple pieces, that you allow enough to get good overlap where the pieces meet and that the ends are tight against the posts. Attach to the inside of the walls with ⅝" #10 screws and fender washers (Figure 3). Take care not to put screws where your back center post will go. Fold down any excess at the top.

Attach the cross-piece. Next, roll the bin onto its back and attach the cross-piece (G) to the bottom of the two front posts. Make sure that the ends of the cross-piece are flush with the outside of the bottom slat. Use four 3" #10 galvanized screws per side. (This will cause the front of your bin to be slightly taller than the back of your bin, but when the completed bin is put in its permanent location, the cross-piece will be nestled into a groove that you will dig into the soil for stability.)

Line the sides of the bin with hardware cloth. Use fender washers and screws and repeat the process described above.

Prepare the center posts. Attach stops (H) to front and back center posts to create slots for the front and divider wall slats to slide into. (You can substitute shorter screws here if you choose.) The back post will need two stops for a slot on one side. The front post will need six stops for slots on three sides (Figure 4). Be sure that you have enough space between stops to allow the ¾" slats to slide up and down.

Attach the back and front center posts. Roll the bin back into its upright position, and place the back center post so that the slot is facing outward to hold the divider wall slats and it is centered on the wall (use the tape measure to determine this). Attach from the outside with screws. Turn bin upside down and center the front center post on the cross-piece so that the three slots will hold the divider wall and front slats. Attach from the bottom with the four 3" galvanized screws (Figure 5). (Having a friend help turn the bin and hold the post will make this much easier!)

Create side slots for the front slats. Attach the remaining four stops (H) to the front corner posts to create additional slots to hold the front panels.

Create front panels. On two of the front slats (B), mark a line 6" in from either end, using a square. Next place a short panel support (J) along each line across the slats so that each slat is flush with the top and bottom of the supports. You should have a 2" gap in between these two slats. Flip the panel over and screw the slats into place. Place the panel in the front of the bin and measure for hardware cloth—it should cover the gap between the slats but not extend into the sliding slot. Attach the hardware cloth with screws and washers (see above). Use the same process to create a wider panel with three more front slats (B) and two long panel supports (K). This time you will leave a 1" gap between slats (Figure 6). Repeat to create a second set of panels for the other side.

Build the divider wall. Attach two spacers (I) each to the bottoms of four divider wall slats (E). Then drop the slats into place. (The lowest one will not need spacers.)

Add the cover piece. Attach the cover piece (F) with the butt hinge on the back wall (Figure 7) and the hasp on the front. This will help hold the front wall in place when your bin is filled with compost.

Attach stationary slats for the lids. First attach the nailers (L) to the sides of the center post so that the tops are flush with the top of the center post. Next place a medium lid slat (M) on the top of the left nailer and the back left corner post and attach. Repeat on the right side.

Build and attach the lids. Assemble each lid by forming a frame out of two medium lid slats (M) and two short lid slats (N) and attaching them using the mending plates and screws. Cut hardware cloth to fit the bottom of the lid and attach with screws and fender washers (Figure 8). Place each lid on the bin so that it overlaps the front slats and sits next to the cover piece. Attach each to a stationary slat with a pair of 1½" × 3" hinges.

Set your bin in place. If you plan to locate your bin on soil, you will want to measure and lay down a piece of hardware cloth on the footprint of your bin. The edges should extend slightly beyond the bottom of your bin. You will also dig a 1½-inch-deep, 7-foot-long groove along the front to accommodate the cross-piece. (Alternately, you can place the bin on a packed gravel base.) You are now ready to start using your bin.

Compost Bench

Cost $460 for cedar; $160 for pine
Time 4 hours
Skill level Advanced

Tools and Supplies

Tape Measure
Pencil
Drill with driving
  attachment

Steel square
Jigsaw
Hand saw
Chisel

Wood

A 4 front slats ¾" × 3 ½" × 43 ½"
B 5 lid seat slats ¾" × 3 ½" × 47 ¾"
C 1 stationary seat slat ¾" × 7" × 48"
D 2 side supports 1 ½" × 3 ½" × 22 ¼"
E 2 tapered back supports,
    1 ½" × 3 ½" × 30 ¼"
F 4 end posts 1 ½" × 3 ½" × 16 ¼"
G 1 cross-piece 1 ½" × 3 ½" × 48"
H 2 armrests, tapered and notched,
    ¾" × 5" × 28 ½"

I 2 curved armrest brackets,
    ¾" × 2 ½" × 5"
J 1 top cap 1 ½" × 3 ½" × 51"
K 1 upper back 1 ½" × 7 ¼" × 51 ½"
L 1 lower back 1 ½" × 3 ½" × 51 ½"
M 8 side slats ¾" × 3 ½" × 26"
N 3 seat cleats 1½" × 3 ½" × 19"
O 4 back slats ¾" × 3 ½" × 48"
P 2 end caps ¾" × ¾" × 16 ¼"
Q 4 stops ¾" × 1 ¼" × 16 ¼"
R 6 spacers for front ¾" × ¾" × 3 ½"

Hardware

2 hinges, 1 ½" × 3"

phillips-head galvanized woodscrews:
    100 @ #10 1½"
    100 @ #12 2½" (for pieces ≥ 1 ½")

Optional (to increase pest resistance):
25' × 3' quarter-inch hardware cloth
50 @ ⅝" #10 screws
50 @ 1" fender washers

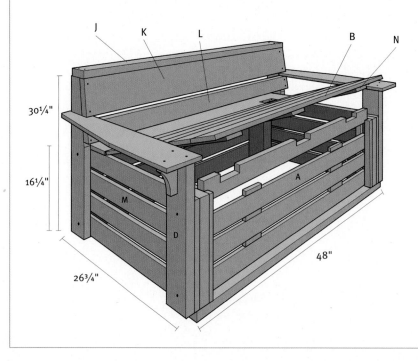

Prepare the front end posts. Attach two stops (Q) and one end cap (P) to one end post (F). The stops will go on the longer side to create a slot for the front slats, and the end cap will go on the opposite side to create a cap for the ends of the side slats. Repeat for the second front end post (Figure 1).

Build the side walls. Each wall will consist of one prepared front end post, four side slats (M), and one additional end post (F). First attach the top and bottom slats to an end post using a square to ensure a right angle (Figure 2). Space two more slats evenly between and attach. Then attach one prepared front end post so that the end cap covers the ends of the slats and the slot is oriented to hold the front slats. Repeat.

Build the back wall. Attach four back slats (O) to one side wall so that they correspond with the side slats. Then attach the second wall in the same way (Figure 3). You will now have a three-sided box.

Finish the base. Attach the cross-piece (G) to the front end posts. Turn the bench over. (Note: The front of your bench will now be slightly taller than the back. When the complete bench is placed in its permanent location, the cross-piece will be nestled into a groove that you will dig for stability.) Lay the stationary seat slat (C) across the back end posts and attach (Figure 4).

Assemble and attach the lid. Attach the three seat cleats (N) to a lid seat slat (B) so that two side cleats are about 5½ inches from the ends and the third is in the center. Place this piece on the base and align another lid seat slat on the cleats so that it is in the proper position to be the front slat and attach (Figure 5). Place the three remaining lid seat slats so that they are evenly spaced and attach. Attach the lid to the stationary seat slat with hinges in line with outer seat cleats.

Assemble the front wall. Slide the bottom front slat (A) into place and screw two spacers (R) into the top edge so that they are equidistant from the ends. Repeat for the next two front slats (Figure 6). Slide the last front slat into place and close the lid to determine proper placement of the notches that will hold the seat cleats. Mark with pencil (Figure 7). Notch the slat with a hand saw and knock out with a chisel. Drop the slat back into place and close the lid.

Attach the side and back supports. Turn the bench on its side. Attach a side support (D) and a back support (E) to the side of the base (Figure 8). The bottoms of the supports should be flush with the bottom edge of the bottom side slat. Repeat on the other side. Turn the bench upright.

Build the backrest. Attach the upper backrest slat (K) to the back arm supports so that the front corners of the slat align with the back corners of the supports. (Ask a helper to hold the slat in place while you attach.) Attach the lower backrest slat (L) to the supports so that it is parallel and evenly spaced between the upper slat and the base. Lay the top cap (J) across the top of the upper slat and supports and attach by screwing in from the top (Figure 9).

Attach the armrests and brackets. Place one armrest (H) on the supports between the backrest slats. In back, screw in to place from the side (Figure 10). In front, screw from the top. Repeat on other side. Place one armrest bracket (I) in the corner formed by the armrest and the support and screw in from the side and top. Repeat on the other side.

Optional: Increase pest resistance. Line the back, sides, and lid with hardware cloth using screws and washers as described on page 56. Close gaps between front slats by omitting spacers and adding an additional ¾" x 2¼" x 43½" slat.

Place your bench. If locating on soil, dig a 1½-inch-deep, 48-inch-long groove to hold the cross-piece. (Lay down a piece of hardware cloth beneath your bin to deter rodents. The edges should extend slightly beyond the bin.) Or place the bin on a packed gravel base and sink the cross-tie in. You are now ready to use your bench.

Indoor Vermicomposting
Mary Appelhof

Even if you lack suitable outdoor space, you can compost food scraps indoors, using worms in small bins. This process is called vermicomposting. These compact composting systems can handle up to five pounds of food scraps each week and generate 10 to 15 gallons of nutrient-rich soil conditioner for gardens and houseplants per year. Vermicomposting offers several advantages over traditional outdoor methods: You can compost indoors and in very small spaces—as little as two cubic feet. The worms also do all the heavy work, turning and aerating the pile. The end product, vermicompost, also has higher nutrient value for plants than compost from a traditional outdoor bin.

To get your worm composting system going, all you need is a suitable container, bedding, redworms, kitchen scraps, and a proper environment. The worms, along with millions of microorganisms, consume food scraps and other organics you bury in moistened bedding and transform it to dark, odorless worm manure called castings. As long as the system has enough oxygen and moisture and remains between freezing and 90°F, the bedding and food scraps vanish, and the worms multiply. You can harvest the vermicompost—a mixture of castings, partially decomposed organics, and uneaten bedding—and use it as topdressing for houseplants, as an ingredient in potting mixes, or as an immediate source of fertilizer for transplants and seed beds. Here's how to start and maintain a system.

Make or Buy Your Bin

All sorts of containers will work as worm bins—but aeration is a must. A common, inexpensive option is a 10- or 12-gallon plastic storage box. Simply drill ten or so quarter-inch holes in the sides, near the top, and another ten in the lid to allow air to circulate (Figure 1, page 67). Some people cover these holes with screening to keep worms and bedding in, but this isn't necessary. Wooden bins with air holes work well too, though they tend to be heavy. You also can purchase commercial vermicomposting units that come with worms and bedding—but these usually end up costing more than building or adapting one yourself and buying your worms separately.

A worm bin allows you to compost indoors, even in tight quarters. It's small enough to stow beneath your kitchen sink but can handle up to five pounds of scraps per week.

Choose Your Bedding

Worm bedding holds moisture and provides worms with a place to live and work. Shredded newspaper is the most common bedding material, and it has the advantage of being readily available and free (Figure 2). For a 12-gallon bin, you will need about five pounds' worth to start.

Machine-shredded office paper, leaf mold, composted horse manure—or some combination of these materials—also make satisfactory low-cost or free bedding. Coconut fiber, also called coir or coco-peat, is often marketed as worm bedding (as well as a growing mix and soil conditioner). It works well too, though it's not cheap. It comes in dry compressed blocks that you place in water—the fiber quickly expands as it absorbs the moisture—before crumbling apart for use. Some vermicomposters recommend peat moss, but this is not a good option. It's too acidic for the worms; furthermore, it's a nonrenewable resource, extracted from bogs at a faster rate than nature can replace it.

Soil is also a component of worm bedding. Worms need small portions—about two to four cups per bin—to provide grit for their gizzards. A loamy soil is ideal for this purpose, but most ordinary garden soils will do just fine. The soil will also inoculate the compost system with bacteria, fungi, and other microorganisms that will create a more diverse group of decomposers than food scraps and bedding alone provide.

Get Your Worms

A successful system requires the right worms for the job—those whose natural tendency is to quickly process large amounts of organics. European redworms (Figure 3) are best suited for this work because they are surface dwellers adapted to feeding on decaying organic matter. They are known variously as redworms, manure worms, red wigglers, and tiger worms, among other common names. To reduce the confusion, use the scientific names for the species, *Eisenia fetida* (these have pronounced stripes) and *E. andrei* (their stripes are less pronounced). Both species process about half their body weight in food per day, reproduce quickly at temperatures between 65°F and 75°F, and can consume a wide range of foods. They do not make extensive burrow systems, so they don't mind being shifted and moved around in the bin as you bury scraps. They don't like bright light and will quickly burrow back under the litter if exposed to the surface. Another European worm sometimes recommended for vermicomposting, *Lumbricus rubellus*, the red earthworm, should be avoided because it has been identified as invasive in some North American forests (see page 71).

Most redworms available from commercial growers are one *Eisenia* species or the other, or a mixture of the two. You can purchase them and other worm-composting supplies at many garden stores and nurseries. You can also find mail-order suppliers online. (See page 104 for additional supplier information.) A one-pound package contains about 1,000 worms, which is the right amount for starting a 12-gallon bin.

Worm Bin Troubleshooting

PROBLEM	CAUSE	SOLUTION
Bad odor	Bin is too wet.	Stop adding water and foods with a high water content; add more dry bedding.
	Bin is not getting enough air.	Turn materials daily. Add paper tubes or bulking agents to create air pockets.
	Choice of food items is inappropriate.	Remove stinky foods. Some foods, like broccoli and onions, take longer to break down and can begin to smell bad in the process.
Fruit flies	Fruit flies may be drawn to fermenting food scraps or may already be present in unwashed fruit peels.	Microwave, freeze or wash food scraps thoroughly in hot water before adding to the bin, or avoid adding fruit until the problem subsides. Bury scraps under a light layer of dry bedding, and try setting a trap (see page 70). If the problem persists, harvest the compost and start a new bin.
Distressed worms	Worms may be drowning because the bin is too wet.	Add more dry bedding and stop adding water.
	Worms may be drying out because the bin is too dry.	Add water regularly, without soaking the bin.
	Worms may be underfed. Once they eat all of their food and bedding, they start eating their castings, which are toxic.	Harvest your compost and replenish your bin with fresh bedding and food scraps.

Don't be tempted to populate your bin with worms from your garden. Most are adapted to life in the mineral layers of the soil and require extensive burrows in order to thrive. Some, like nightcrawlers (*Lumbricus terrestris*), feed on the surface but live deep underground. These worms are ill suited to the shallow environment of a worm bin. They also don't process as much organic material as redworms and won't reproduce quickly in a bin, if at all.

Assemble the System

Once you have your container, bedding, and redworms, all you need is water and about a quart of chopped fruit and vegetable scraps to start your bin. Put the shredded paper in the bin, add the soil, and then add around two gallons of water (Figure 4), mixing until most of the paper is moistened. It should be damp but not wringing wet. (If the paper crinkles, it's too dry). Empty the worms and the medium they were packaged in on top of the bedding; they will quickly move down into the paper away from the light. Draw enough bedding aside to make room for the produce scraps and dump them into the hole. Spread bedding over the scraps, put the lid on the container, and place it in any convenient indoor location. Many people keep their bins in the kitchen under the sink, but the laundry room or basement also works. Some space-starved composters have even been known to store them under the bed!

Feed Your Worms and Maintain Your Bin

Your worms will need about three to five pounds of food per week (depending on how fast they multiply), and you can feed them as often as daily or as infrequently as weekly. All kinds of organic material can work as worm food, but most people have the best luck with vegetable and fruit scraps, tea leaves, coffee grounds (bags and filters work too), and eggshells (which add calcium and other nutrients; pulverize them first to hasten decomposition). You can also add citrus rinds, but only in small amounts—large doses cause odors and can kill the worm population. Avoid highly acidic foods (for example, those containing lots of vinegar), as well as meat, bones, and dairy products, all of which will cause odors and attract flies, rats, or other pests. Add your scraps in different spots in the bin (Figure 5) and cover with a light layer of bedding to minimize odors. After several weeks you'll notice that the food scraps are disappearing, some faster than others.

Monitor the bedding regularly for adequate moisture. Remember, it should feel like a wrung-out sponge. If it's dry, add water with a watering can or mister. If it's too wet, add more dry bedding. You will also notice that your worms will reproduce. The first sign will be yellowish cocoons, each somewhat smaller than a mung bean. After two or three months, you may have twice as many worms as you started with. Please do not release the extras in natural areas! Instead, help a

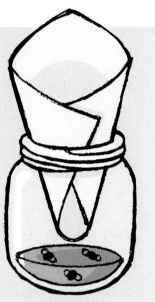

Farewell to Fruit Flies

If fruit flies are plaguing your worm bin, try setting a simple trap. Pour about an inch of beer or apple cider into a jar or bottle, or just use a wine bottle and leave the dregs. Add a few drops of dish detergent, ideally one with a fruity scent. Then make a paper cone with a small opening at the bottom and secure it with tape. Place the cone in the bottle or jar so that it fits snugly inside and is suspended above the liquid. Fruit flies will smell the beer, wine or cider, and fly into the cone. Most will drown because the detergent breaks the surface tension of the liquid. Any others will be trapped inside the jar.

neighbor set up a bin, or just leave them be. Worm populations will die back if there is not enough food, so overpopulation will not be a problem.

Collect and Use the Castings

When the material in the bin becomes dark and crumbly (usually in three to six months), it's ready to use. You can separate the vermicompost from the worms by hand, taking as much as two thirds of it at once. Or push all of the contents to one side of your bin (Figure 6) and add fresh bedding to the other side. Start adding scraps to the fresh side, and after about a month, the worms will have migrated over, leaving the mature compost largely worm free and easy to collect.

Use your finished vermicompost as topdressing on your houseplants or as an ingredient in potting mixes. My favorite use is to deposit a handful in the hole when transplanting vegetables such as broccoli and tomatoes. This places the vermicompost nutrients right in the root zone of the developing plant. Plants fertilized with worm castings thrive, providing beauty, pleasure, and (in the case of veggies) good food. Then the cycle continues as the trimmings from these plants are put back in the worm bin to be recycled again in a convenient, natural, and environmentally sound way.

Worms Running Wild

Niall Dunne

Gardeners almost always think of earthworms as beneficial. They help plow, aerate, hydrate, and fertilize the earth. In the words of Charles Darwin, "they mingle the whole intimately together." But some species, when placed in the wrong context, can become outright pests. These earthworms have invaded hardwood forests in the northern U.S. and are harming native plant and animal communities there.

In a healthy northern forest, a layer of decomposing leaf litter covers the ground, providing nutrients for plants and a medium for seedlings. This duff layer also acts as mulch and provides habitat for insects and other invertebrates. Invasive earthworms feed voraciously on leaf litter, breaking it down too fast and allowing valuable nutrients to leach through the soil. Some worm species also carry organic matter deep into the mineral layers of the soil, placing nutrients out of the reach of many plants. The decrease in leaf litter also allows the soil to dry out. The drier, more nutrient-deficient soil that results is less suited for many native plants. All of these changes affect animals up and down the food chain. Making matters worse, the changes in soil can pave the way for pest plants like garlic mustard.

Invasive worms weren't introduced by vermicomposting. They arrived over the past several hundred years through the dumping of fish bait and dry ship ballast, and more recently via imported plants. But since they are wreaking such havoc, vermicomposters should be mindful of what's in their bins. European redworms (*Eisenia fetida* and *E. andrei*), the two species predominantly sold for composting, are rusty brown with alternating yellow and maroon bands. They have eight bristles, or setae, arranged in pairs around each segment (Figure A). They have established themselves in the wild here but so far have not been identified as a problem. However, batches of *Eisenia* may harbor Asian *Amynthas* species, which are highly invasive here. *Amynthas* are reddish brown, unbanded, and very active, hence their common name jumping worms. They have numerous bristles all around each segment (Figure B). Another European compost species, *Lumbricus rubellus*, is also causing trouble, and it is easily confused with *Eisenia* species. It lacks bands and is dark red with a light yellow underside but has the same setal pattern.

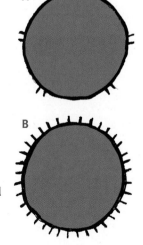

A

B

That said, making an ID is difficult for a nonexpert. To be on the safe side, forest ecologists now advise vermicomposters—especially those near noninfested natural areas—to freeze castings in airtight bags for at least a week before using them in the garden, no matter what species they have. Doing so won't hurt the beneficial soil microbes, but it will kill the worms and cocoons.

Worms in the Classroom

Ashley Gamell

Earthworms hold a special fascination for children, and this makes them both fun and functional classroom companions. Vermicomposting at school provides a wealth of learning opportunities in science and sustainability for children of all grades and abilities. Young students enjoy observing worm life cycles and behavior, while older students can tackle more advanced topics like earthworm anatomy and waste reduction. Having a worm bin in the class also helps kids develop problem-solving skills and engages them in team building and stewardship as they work together to care for the wiggliest of class pets.

Setting up and managing a worm bin is relatively easy and inexpensive. (See the previous chapter for general how-to information.) It doesn't take up much room, and since compost worms need a dark environment, you can locate your bin inside a closed cupboard or under a desk. One pound of red wigglers (*Eisenia fetida*) will be enough to start your bin and should cost approximately $25. You can order them online, but if possible, it's best to pick them up in person and introduce them to their new home as soon as possible.

A bin of red wigglers will eat upwards of three pounds of food scraps per week. You can provide them in daily feedings or add as much as a whole week's worth to the bin at once, say, in preparation for school breaks. As long as they have enough food, worms can be left unattended for a week or more—just make sure to mist the bin generously before you go. They won't make it through summer vacation, however, so plan to take them home or recruit a student willing to adopt them at the end of the school year. Here are some tips for teachers on using a worm bin in the classroom.

Involve Students in Managing the Bin

Procure a plastic storage tub and enlist your students in adapting it, collecting and shredding newspaper for bedding, and introducing your first batch of worms. Assign a student "worm monitor" for each day of the week, giving them responsibility for maintaining your clew (as a group of worms is called). The worm monitor can check on and adjust the bin's moisture level and supervise the addition of food scraps. He or she might also chart data such as odor and pH (redworms do best when it is close

Children are always fascinated with worms. A classroom vermicomposting bin offers a host of opportunities to teach real-world lessons that take advantage of their natural curiosity.

to neutral), or weigh how much food goes into the bin. All the students can work together to measure population changes with a monthly worm count.

When it's time to harvest the castings, students can work in teams to separate the compost from the worms using the "mound" technique: Simply dump the contents of the bin on a table, arrange into small mounds, and suspend a light above the table. The worms will gradually move inward, away from the light, allowing students to remove the compost from the outside of the piles. Older students may be able to devise their own harvesting methods based on what they learn about worm behavior. (What are worms attracted to? Repelled by?) Though some students may initially resist the idea of handling the castings, most will come around when they discover they are totally odorless and look merely like rounded soil particles.

Use your vermicompost in the classroom where you can continue to study its value. For example, you could stage a simple experiment comparing the growth rates of seedlings planted in vermicompost-enriched soil with those planted in other potting mixes. If there is extra, the class can vote on whether to donate it to a neighboring class, a community garden, or a park.

Make Your Worms a Subject of Study

Worms are captivating specimens. They have five hearts but no eyes, breathe through their skin, and reside in a mysterious world underneath our feet. Spread samples from the worm bin on cafeteria trays and invite students to gently explore using plastic spoons and magnifying glasses. Evidence of the whole worm life cycle can be found inside the bin. Have your students hunt for yellow worm cocoons and tiny "baby" worms. Have small groups of students observe single worms, keeping the critters moist using damp paper towels. Ask students to notice how the worms move, feel, and respond to stimuli. Encourage them to generate their own research questions.

Worms play a vital role in many ecosystems, digesting organic matter, making nutrients available to plants, and aerating the soil. Ask your students to close their eyes and imagine what a forest might look like without decomposers to consume and process fallen leaves and dead plants year after year. Take them outside and ask them to gather a rotting log as well as a few trays of leaf litter to examine. What kinds of decomposers are at work? Digging deeper into the soil, the students may find other species of worms that they can compare with the red wigglers in the classroom bin.

Explore Waste and Sustainability

The decomposition process inside a worm bin is very different from the smelly type we associate with landfills. Students can investigate the difference between aerobic composting and the anaerobic decomposition that happens in a buried landfill by sealing food scraps inside small zip-lock bags and observing the contents over several weeks. How does this process compare with what's happening in your worm bin?

The entire life cycle of a worm can be found in a bin. Sending students on a hunt for worm cocoons will foster a real sense of discovery.

Explore how decomposition affects other kinds of trash by adding dated samples of plastic, tinfoil, cardboard, and wood to your bin and tracking what happens to them over time. Do they change in a week? A year? Begin a conversation about waste by having students sort the trash left over from their lunches into biodegradable and nonbiodegradable materials. Extend the lesson by challenging your students to plan a lunch together that is completely compostable, and have a vermi-picnic!

Turn Problems into Teaching Opportunities

Managing a worm bin inevitably involves some problem solving. When you notice an issue, use it as an opportunity for developing critical-thinking skills. Have your class develop hypotheses about the cause of the problem and brainstorm a solution. For instance, if the worm bin begins to smell "rotten," you might delve into a productive discussion about anaerobic bacteria and research the kinds of conditions that may have led to the problem (see page 68 for hints). Your worm bin will also likely become host to other critters that your class can investigate, from pesky fruit flies to large, pretty soldier flies. Whether beneficial or problematic, everything that happens in your worm bin can be a catalyst for learning. Your worm bin is a miniature ecosystem, with dynamic natural processes at play. Look at it as a science experiment, and follow your class's curiosity wherever it leads you.

Using Compost in the Garden
Miranda Smith

Good-quality compost benefits the soil and plants in your garden in ways that no other amendment can. You can use it as a soil conditioner, a fertilizer, a weed-suppressing mulch—or all three at once. You can also use it to brew compost tea, which can then be used as a soil drench or sprayed on plant leaves to battle foliar diseases (see "Compost Tea for the Home Gardener," page 86). In addition, compost is one of the primary ingredients in most good potting soil mixes.

Not all composts are created equal. Three factors determine the qualities of compost: the initial ingredients, the type of composting process used, and the length of time and conditions under which the compost cured. To some extent, you can customize your compost to fit your needs by simply changing one or another of these elements. For example, vermicompost made primarily with food scraps is particularly rich in nutrients and makes a good fertilizer, while a compost that contains a high proportion of leaves is lightweight and makes a good mulch.

Whatever you plan to do with your compost, first make sure it is ready for use. Unfinished compost can damage your plants by robbing nitrogen from the soil and retarding growth. Finished compost is dark brown, crumbly, and earthy smelling, and it bears no resemblance to its original components. The temperature of finished compost is roughly the same as that of the surrounding air temperature, and the pile should not heat up when turned or aerated. You can check to see if your compost is cured using simple, informal tests such as the plastic bag test and the cress test (see the following page); in general, if your compost is still warm, smells like ammonia, or contains a lot of recognizable original material, it needs more time to mature. Once it is ready, you can apply it in a number of ways.

Soil Conditioner for New Plantings

Garden plants need a balance of air and water in the soil to ensure healthy growth. All composts—regardless of original ingredients, composting process, and length of curing phase—help provide this balance by improving soil structure. Compost promotes the formation of loose, granular aggregates in the soil, enhancing its permeability to air and water as well as its water-holding capacity. If your soil is too

Compost can be worked in as a soil conditioner for new plantings or spread on the soil surface for established ones.

Is Your Compost Ready to Use?

The simplest way to find out if your compost is finished is to conduct a "bag test." Put a handful of compost in a zip-lock bag and leave it in there for a week or so. Then open the bag and sniff. If you smell ammonia or sourness instead of a pleasant earthy odor, the microorganisms in your compost are still at work and you need to let it mature. Try it again in several weeks.

Or try the "cress test." Cress (*Lepidium sativa*) is very susceptible to phytotoxins, but given healthy growing conditions, it germinates at a very high rate in only four or five days. Fill two flats with media—one with straight compost and the other with a conventional potting mixture as a control. Plant each of the flats with 25 cress seeds, water, cover with plastic, and wait for them to germinate. Track the number of sprouts in each flat. If you get close to 100 percent germination in the control but fewer than 20 seedlings in the compost-filled flat, your compost is probably not yet ready for use.

sandy, adding compost will improve water and nutrient retention; if it's too clayey, compost will help improve airflow and drainage and make the soil easier to work with a fork or shovel. Compost can also help rebuild the structure and vitality of soils that have been damaged by compaction and erosion.

When preparing a new planting bed for annuals or perennials in a garden with poor soil, amend the soil to a depth of six to eight inches by adding an inch or two of finished compost. Begin when the ground is moderately moist, spread the desired amount of compost evenly over the soil surface with a rake, and then turn it under using a square-tined fork. Never work the soil when it's wet because this can lead to compaction; digging the soil when it's too dry can cause loss of structure. Avoid using a rototiller, which can also compact your soil.

If you already have good-quality garden soil, then there's no need to dig in your compost. Just apply it as mulch to the surface (see next page). Earthworms and other organisms will gradually incorporate the compost into the soil, improving its structure. This "no-till" approach to conditioning is becoming more and more popular with gardeners—even those with poor soils or who maintain annual beds or vegetable patches—for good reason. It's less work, and it also prevents damage to mycorrhizal fungi and other beneficial organisms in the soil. It also reduces the carbon footprint of gardening by sequestering carbon underground. Disturbing soil allows soil bacteria to rapidly oxidize the carbon locked in organic matter and vent it into the atmosphere as carbon dioxide.

When planting a tree or shrub, most experts now advise against amending your planting hole. Adding compost or other organic amendments to the soil before backfilling the hole may discourage the plant's roots from spreading out and developing a strong, stable root system. It's better to plant your tree or shrub in your garden's native soil and finish by spreading an inch of compost on top of the back-filled hole and covering it with a layer of coarse mulch like wood chips.

Compost as Mulch

For gardens with established plants, digging in compost is not recommended, as this can damage delicate surface roots. Instead, apply your compost as mulch or topdressing by spreading it over the soil surface. This will deliver a healthy dose of organic matter that will also moderate soil temperatures, mitigate erosion, and retain moisture. A thick layer will also suppress weeds.

Any finished compost can be applied in this way, but those made primarily from leaves and other yard waste are the best choices because of their lighter texture. Unlike mulches composed of wood chips and pine needles, which are added in deep layers, compost should be applied only an inch or two deep, since it's much finer. If it's laid on too thickly, it will prevent air from reaching the soil and may smother tree roots. Use a wheelbarrow to transport large amounts of compost around the garden and a rake to spread it evenly over the soil surface.

Each spring after the soil has warmed and again in early fall, apply compost to vegetable gardens and other annual beds, as well as near the bases of woody plants. Take care not to pile the compost "volcano style" against the trunks of trees and shrubs; this can promote fungal decay of bark and provide a home for pest animals.

Adding compost to new planting areas will condition poor soil and increase fertility. Dig in one to two inches of compost for every six to eight inches of soil.

Also avoid mulching with compost that may carry viable weed seeds, which can germinate once they're exposed to sunlight. Use hot-composted mulch, or better yet, avoid adding seeds to your pile in the first place. Keep finished compost covered to keep out windborne weed seeds.

Compost as a Slow-Release Fertilizer

Not all the materials in compost are fully broken down by the time it is considered "finished." When you spread it on soil, you are adding a diverse population of microorganism decomposers as well as food supplies for them. As these organisms continue the decay process, they slowly release nutrients into the soil, making them available for absorption by plant roots.

Keep in mind that compared with synthetic fertilizers, compost contains a modest supply of the primary plant nutrients nitrogen (N), phosphorus (P), and potassium (K). However, because the nutrients in compost are released slowly, its effects last longer, and there is a lower risk of nutrients leaching from the soil and contaminating groundwater. Compost is also a rich source of secondary nutrients and trace elements missing from synthetics.

Composts vary in the types and amounts of nutrients they contain, depending on their base ingredients. A compost made from leaves and yard trimmings is likely to be high in trace elements, for example, and low in available N, P, and K.

Apply an inch or two of compost to your garden twice a year, once in the spring, before new planting (left), and again in the fall. Use a rake to spread it evenly over the surface.

How much compost should I use?

Here are guidelines on how much compost you might use for various purposes.

New planting beds (annual or perennial herbaceous plants) or new lawns	1" to 2" worked into top 6" to 8" of soil
New trees and shrubs	1" spread over the backfilled planting hole
Established beds	1" to 2" spread uniformly over surface, twice a year (spring and fall)
Existing lawns	⅛" to ¼" spread uniformly over grass (or use compost tea)
Established trees and shrubs	1" to 2" spread beneath the canopy, twice a year (spring and fall)
Potting soil	1:3 to 1:2 compost to soil mix

How much should I buy?

If you are purchasing compost, first determine how many cubic yards you'll need. Measure the square footage of the relevant areas, determine how deep you will dress them, and use the table below. Compost is typically sold by the cubic yard or in 40-pound bags. A cubic yard of compost weighs roughly 1,000 pounds.

Area / Depth	¼" deep	½" deep	1" deep	1½" deep
100 sq. ft.	.08 cubic yards (roughly 80 lbs.)	.16 cubic yards (160 lbs.)	.32 cubic yards (320 lbs.)	.48 cubic yards (480 lbs.)
500 sq. ft.	.40 cubic yards (400 lbs.)	.80 cubic yards (800 lbs.)	1.6 cubic yards (1,600 lbs.)	3.1 cubic yards (3,100 lbs.)
1,000 sq. ft.	.80 cubic yards (800 lbs.)	1.6 cubic yards (1,600 lbs.)	3.2 cubic yards (3,200 lbs.)	6.2 cubic yards (6,200 lbs.)

Generally, the best composts for use as fertilizers have a high proportion of manure and/or kitchen scraps. And the more diverse the original ingredients, the more complete the resulting nutrient supply.

Over time, as more and more of the active organic matter in the compost breaks down, the rate of nutrient release slows. Eventually, the remaining material (humus), will be relatively resistant to further decay. At this point, it will not be a source of nutrients, though it will continue to condition the soil—improving its ability to hold air and moisture and exchange nutrients—thereby stimulating plant growth.

Applying one to two inches of compost per year to the soil surface will slowly build up the store of organic matter and provide a reservoir of nutrients that should suffice for most garden plants. If you have a vegetable garden and grow a lot of heavy feeders (annuals with high nutrient demands) such as broccoli, corn, squash, or tomatoes, you may need to supplement this annual compost application. You can side-dress with a half-inch layer of compost each month or apply a natural fertilizer such as alfalfa pellets or fish meal that provides a more immediate source of plant nutrients.

It's important to use only finished compost—or you may end up depriving your plants of nitrogen. Compost made with a large fraction of well-shredded carbonaceous materials such as autumn leaves or sawdust bedding can seem finished before it is. Because the carbon content is so high, these composts frequently run out of nitrogen before all the carbonaceous materials have been broken down.

Consequently, they seem finished because they don't reheat after being turned. If you dig unfinished, high-carbon compost into your garden soil, its decomposers will scavenge nitrogen from the immediate environment to sustain themselves while they complete the composting process. In this way, they may end up borrowing nutrients from your plants rather than contributing them. Eventually, the balance of nutrients will return, but your plants may suffer in the meantime.

Compost weighs about 37 pounds per cubic foot. A wheelbarrow will help you transport large amounts around your garden.

Some vegetables, like squash, have high nutrient demands and may need a monthly application of compost as a boost during the growing season.

That said, there is one instance in which it's okay to use compost that hasn't yet cured. If in the fall you find yourself with a pile of unfinished compost and no place to store it over the winter, you can use it to fertilize a bare vegetable patch in preparation for spring planting.

Simply pull up any remaining plants, and then apply a half inch or less of your uncured compost. Work it into the soil, and then sow a cover crop such as clover. You could also spread uncured compost over a vigorously growing cover crop and let the rain and snow work it into the soil over the winter. By spring the compost will have matured and will be ready to contribute nutrients and improve the tilth of your garden.

Compost in Potting Soil

Compost added to a potting-soil mix promotes healthy plant growth by enhancing the soil's water-holding capacity and fertility. It also supplies the potting mix with populations of beneficial bacteria and fungi. A recipe of one third compost, one third expanded coconut fiber (also called coir or coco peat), one sixth vermiculite, and one sixth perlite will provide a balanced supply of nutrients as well as good drainage and water retention to most indoor and outdoor container plants for at least six weeks.

Potting soil containing one third to one quarter compost will help nourish an outdoor container garden or houseplants.

It's imperative to use high-quality compost in any potting-soil mix. Only use fully finished, screened material: Some of the by-products that form during the composting process are phytotoxic, or poisonous to plants—but these are no longer present in properly cured compost.

Be sure to avoid compost that might contain weed seeds or diseased plant material. Most seeds and pathogens are killed during the hot composting method. You can also pasteurize your soil mix by baking it in the oven in a tightly covered pot at 180°F for 30 minutes; however, this process will likely kill beneficial organisms in the growing medium.

Shopping Tips: How to Choose the Best Commercial Compost

Rod Tyler

You can buy commercially made compost at garden centers, nurseries, or farmers' markets. Some municipalities even give it away. Most are made primarily either of yard trimmings, cow or chicken manure, or worm castings. No matter what the original ingredients, here's how to find a good batch.

Investigate what's in the bag. Run the compost through your hands. Does it smell earthy, like soil? If so, it's stable and ready for use. If it smells vinegary or of ammonia, it needs to cure more. Also make sure that it's not hot to the touch. A fully finished compost will be the same temperature as the air. The original ingredients should be nearly unrecognizable. If the compost is made from leaves, you shouldn't see leaf bits in the finished compost. Likewise, if the compost is made from twigs and branches, none should be visible after it has been screened for sale; half-inch-grade compost is the most widely useful texture and can be used for anything from top-dressing a lawn to enhancing the soil in a flower bed.

Consider the color. Most cured composts are very dark brown to black and consistent in color throughout the batch. (There are some exceptions to this rule. Chicken manure compost, for example, is normally lighter in color.)

Read the label. Look for compost with a fertilizer analysis (N-P-K value) of at least 1-.5-.5 to 1-1-1. The numbers may seem low, but the compost will release more nutrients over time, and you'll be adding organic matter to the soil.

Ask about salt content. Make sure that the soluble salts in the compost fall below the level deemed safe for the plants you intend to grow. For example, many tender annuals are salt sensitive and may suffer from "transplanting shock"—actually a slight burn from the salts. (Salt levels should be at least below five millimhos per centimeter.)

Research before buying in bulk. If you're planning a big project with compost, consider asking your supplier the following questions: Can you provide directions for proper use of the compost for my specific needs? Is a steady, consistent supply on hand at all times? Has the compost been used in any local projects? Can you custom mix compost to meet my needs?

Compost Tea for the Home Gardener
Joshua Cohen

A traditional practice that has been gaining a lot of traction is the brewing and application of compost tea. In the old days, compost tea was a simple liquid extract made by putting some finished compost in a burlap sack and letting it steep in water for a while. The resulting brew, rich in plant minerals and other beneficial compounds, was then used as a root drench or foliar spray to deliver some of the fertilizing and disease-suppressing chemistry of solid compost directly and quickly to garden plants.

In recent years, the brewing process has become more high-tech. Practitioners use aeration equipment to provide a constant flow of oxygen to the mix in order to nurture diverse cultures of compost microorganisms in the tea. This "actively aerated compost tea" is used not only to fertilize plants and reduce the incidence of foliar diseases but also to inoculate and revitalize the soil with populations of beneficial bacteria, fungi, protozoa, and nematodes, thereby enhancing the entire soil food web.

Compost tea does not supply all the benefits of solid compost, such as directly building your soil's supply of organic matter and improving its structure, but there are certain circumstances in which it can make sense to convert your compost into liquid form. If you only have a small amount of compost but a large area of soil in need of amendment, brewing compost tea is a way to maximize your compost resources and perform a more widespread application. It's also easier to confer the benefits of compost to a lawn or large mulched bed if you're able to spray the stuff on. In addition, compost tea can add key plant nutrients and beneficial microbes to soil without adding additional bulk, which might be a concern for rooftop, balcony, or other container gardens.

The Basics of Brewing

Modern compost tea brewers are designed to introduce air into a solution of compost and water. Aeration helps loosen microorganisms from the organic components and encourages optimal growth of beneficial aerobic microbes. In contrast, nonaerated teas are less biologically active and may contain harmful anaerobic pathogens.

Compost tea delivers some of the benefits of compost in liquid form, which can make it easier to apply to lawns and rooftop gardens.

A homemade compost tea aeration system can be fashioned from a bucket and basic aquarium supplies: a pump, a bubbler, plastic tubing, and a valve.

A large selection of brewers can be found for sale online or at garden centers, from inexpensive bucket kits to pricey commercial tank systems. (See the resources section on page 103 for supplier information.) It's also very easy to build your own brewer: All you need is a bucket (a five-gallon plastic one will work well), a fine-mesh bag or nylon stocking for holding the compost, and some basic aquarium supplies: a pump, an air stone or "bubbler," a gang valve, and several feet of plastic or rubber tubing.

Set up your brewer in a location that's out of direct sunlight and close to an electrical outlet, which you'll need to run the pump. Fill the bucket with water, leaving a few inches of space at the top for bubbling. Connect the pump and bubbler using the plastic tubing, and put the bubbler at the bottom of the bucket. If you are using municipal water or think the water has been chlorinated, aerate it by turning on the pump for a couple of hours to dissipate the chlorine and other additives, which can kill off the beneficial microbes you wish to nurture.

Add about four cups of high-quality finished compost to the mesh bag. (The ratio of compost to water can vary slightly. This won't affect the concentration of your tea enough to make any difference in the way you will use it.) Tie the bag closed and lower it into the water, again allowing room at the top for bubbling. Aerate the tea continuously for 24 to 36 hours at room temperature. Check the brewer a few times a day to make sure the pump is working, and give the tea a stir using a stick each time you visit. It's best to use the compost tea as soon as possible after brewing, so plan accordingly. For instance, make sure you have the time and necessary equipment, like a watering can or pump sprayer, to apply it promptly.

Tailoring Teas for Different Plants

The ratio of fungi to bacteria varies in different soils throughout the natural world. In general, fungi tend to dominate in forest soils, while bacterial biomass is higher in prairies and agricultural soils. Based on these differences, some compost tea makers aim to create fungal-dominated compost tea for trees, shrubs, and perennials and bacterial-dominated batches for grasses, vegetable crops, and other annuals.

One way to do this is by customizing the original components of the compost used to make the tea. To create a bacterial-dominated compost, you need to use a much higher ratio of green material to brown material; to create a fungal-dominated compost, there should be a preponderance of brown ingredients. Another option is to customize your formula with additives that favor either fungal or bacterial growth. (Or you could do both.) Nutrient sources such as molasses, sea kelp, or fish emulsion encourage larger populations of beneficial microorganisms, and different additives stimulate different organisms. For example, sea kelp contains nutrients for bacteria, and flour encourages the growth of beneficial fungi. (See "Two Compost Tea Recipes," page 91.)

Compost Tea and Disease Prevention

There is strong, documented evidence that solid compost used as a mulch has the ability to suppress numerous soil-borne diseases. And there is a fair amount of peer-reviewed research supporting the effectiveness of old-fashioned, nonaerated compost tea at reducing the incidence of plant foliar diseases such as powdery mildew. Using aerated compost tea to suppress disease, though, is a relatively new practice, and hard research on it is just getting under way. Many claims about its effectiveness are based on anecdotal evidence or are found in reports in non-peer-reviewed publications.

In formal trials, results have often been mixed or inconsistent. For example, some research has found aerated tea to be somewhat effective against powdery mildew and gray mold but ineffective at suppressing black rot and downy mildew. More scientific research will no doubt be conducted as compost tea grows in popularity. In the meantime, gardeners can conduct their own informal experiments.

Do be careful not to overuse your compost tea. It contains a high concentration of easily assimilated nutrients, and if your plants absorb too much of them, they might become susceptible to attack by diseases and pests. If your plants begin to show signs of nutrient excess such as weak, sappy growth, leaves that are too large and lush, or unusual attractiveness to aphids, cut back on your compost tea application.

A word of caution about using additives, however: Some sugar-rich additives, especially molasses, can stimulate the growth of *E. coli* and other human pathogens that may be present in low concentrations in the compost. To avoid this risk, if you use compost tea in your vegetable garden, the U.S. Department of Agriculture recommends that you only use potable water in the brewing phase, regularly sanitize your equipment, and either avoid additives or stop applying compost tea made with additives three to four months prior to harvesting your edibles. You can also lower the risk of contamination by using compost produced by the hot method and avoiding any made with animal manures.

Applying Compost Tea

Ideally, you should use your compost tea within two hours of completing the brewing process, while it is still teeming with live microorganisms. If you wait longer, conditions in the tea will become less favorable to beneficial aerobic microbes and they'll quickly start to die off. Pour the finished liquid into a watering can or pump sprayer for application. (You can add the remaining compost solids back onto the compost pile.) Clean your brewing equipment after each completed batch with a solution of one part chlorine bleach and nine parts water, and then rinse it thoroughly with fresh water.

Compost tea can be applied with a pump sprayer. Ideally, this should happen within two hours of completing the brewing process, so plan accordingly.

Two Compost Tea Recipes

Christopher Roddick

You can encourage the growth of either fungi or bacteria in your tea by varying the initial ingredients. Here are recipes for two teas, one a fungi-rich brew for woody plants, the other a bacteria-rich tea for herbaceous plants. You can find the additives you need in a garden supply store, except where otherwise noted.

For Trees and Shrubs

7 cups good-quality mature compost, placed in mesh bag

About 4 gallons chlorine-free water

½ cup infant oatmeal (found in the baby food aisle of grocery stores)

1½ teaspoons unsulfured molasses (found in grocery stores)

1–2 tablespoons sea kelp

1–2 tablespoons fish hydrolysate

2 tablespoons humic acid

For Herbaceous Plants

5 cups good-quality mature compost, placed in mesh bag

About 4 gallons chlorine-free water

2–3 tablespoons unsulfured molasses

2–3 tablespoons sea kelp

2 tablespoons fish hydrolysate

1½ teaspoons vegetable oil

Instructions

Add water to a bucket outfitted with aerating pump, leaving enough space to accommodate compost and additives and still leave a few inches for bubbling. Add compost and other ingredients. Aerate for 24 to 36 hours at 70°F to 75°F, stirring occasionally. Remove compost bag. (You can put the solids back in your compost pile.) Use the finished tea as soon as possible as a soil drench or foliar spray. If using as a foliar spray, a tablespoon of molasses added to the finished tea will help it stick to leaves.

You can apply compost tea as often as once a week either as a soil drench, by pouring it directly around the root zones of your plants (especially useful after transplanting), or as a foliar spray, applied directly onto plant leaves.

No matter what formula or application method you start with, use some trial and error to see what works best for your garden. You don't have to worry, say, that adding a fungal-based tea to your lawn will cause harm. As long as you brew your tea using good-quality finished compost made from a variety of greens and browns, you'll end up with a diverse mix of beneficial microorganisms.

Composting in the City

Jennifer Blackwell

Composting in a dense urban area presents a number of challenges. Space is tight, which can make setting up and managing a pile difficult, and leaves and other browns are in short supply. Of course a major challenge is the presence of rats and other urban-adapted animals that view a compost pile as a food source or place to live. Our fellow human beings can also frustrate our efforts—not everyone is eager to have a compost pile located nearby. Following is advice on how to cope and be a successful city composter.

Rodent-Proofing Your Pile

If you are composting food waste, take steps to ensure that rodents and other critters don't mistake your compost pile for an all-night buffet. Raccoons, rats, mice, and even curious feral cats can make a mess of your compost or decide to take up residence in or around your compost area. Because wild animals in urban areas are always looking for warm, moist places to nest, even gardeners who stick to composting leaves, garden trimmings, and wood chips need to consider animal-proofing their pile. Here are some basic tips.

Avoid problem ingredients. Dairy products, fish and meat scraps or bones, and fatty or oily foods are magnets for rats and other pests. When you add food scraps of any kind to your pile, bury them deep inside it in order to minimize odors. Make sure you have the proper balance of brown and green ingredients, and always leave a two-inch covering of browns on top of your compost pile. The barrier of browns will help soak up excess moisture and prevent odors of decomposition from escaping, making your pile less attractive to rodents.

Protect your pile. Consider using a steel trash-can composter with tiny holes drilled in the sides, bottom, and top—the most rodent-resistant bin available. Alternately, line your existing bin with heavy-gauge galvanized half- or quarter-inch hardware cloth. Make sure there are no gaps in the cloth—rodents are smarter than you think and will look for weaknesses in the barrier!

Who says you need a garden to compost? Many city dwellers bring their food scraps to public collection sites, like those run by GrowNYC at greenmarkets in Brooklyn.

Clean up your garden and composting area. Rodents love clutter because it provides them with convenient places to hide and small reservoirs of collected rainwater. You may also want to rip out any heavy groundcovers in your garden, especially ivy—premium habitat for rats and other burrowers. Rats and mice don't like open spaces and tend to travel along walls, so keep your compost bin at least a foot away from walls and corners. Also, install an impenetrable barrier underneath your bin to keep rodents from nesting beneath it or burrowing in from below. One way to do this is by pouring a square of permeable concrete for your pile to rest on. Another is to place a foundation of cinder blocks a foot deep into the soil so that your bin sits flush with the ground. Fill the cinder blocks with crushed gravel and sand so that even tiny mice can't get through.

Sourcing Browns

Run out of dried leaves for your compost? Most urban areas have no shortage of high-nitrogen greens in the form of food waste, but finding a steady supply of high-carbon browns in the city can be tricky. Get creative and look for untapped sources of brown materials in your neighborhood that might otherwise be headed to the landfill.

If you live in an area with a lot of deciduous street trees, hoard fallen leaves for composting year-round. Ask neighbors and managers of nearby parks for their leaves too. In addition, find out how your city manages its tree and park waste. Many municipalities have free wood chips that you can pick up from a centralized location. For example, in Brooklyn, Green-Wood Cemetery provides year-round access to wood chips. New York City's annual MulchFest event invites residents to bring their Christmas trees to city parks to have them chipped and bagged for use as mulch or in compost.

See if there's a natural wood shop in or near your neighborhood, and ask the owner if you can take home unwanted sawdust or wood shavings (from untreated lumber only). Partner with your local coffee or cacao roasters to recycle their waste: the chaff (shells) from the coffee and cacao beans is a fragrant, small-particle-size brown that has a low C:N ratio compared with woodier materials. (Not to be confused with fresh grounds, which count as greens because of their high nitrogen content.)

Use leftover straw bales from autumnal store displays or Halloween parties. Horse stables might also give away moldy hay or stable bedding—which is great for the compost pile (though be aware that hay can harbor weed seeds). You can also add shredded newspaper or brown paper bags to your compost pile. Just don't fill up your entire bin with paper—it clumps and compacts easily.

Home Composting in Small Spaces

Composting on your own in the city can be difficult, especially since space is at a premium. Maximize your available space by building compost towers, using garden

High-carbon materials can be scarce in cities. Many urban gardeners cope by stockpiling dry leaves in the fall and adding them to their piles as the need arrives.

furniture that doubles as a bin, or vermicomposting indoors. Remember, you can make compost just about anywhere in your home, even on a rooftop or balcony.

Go vertical. Instead of devoting a separate area of your garden to a large compost pile, you can save space by integrating one or more tall, slender compost towers among your garden plants. A compost tower is just a narrow column of chicken wire, wire mesh, or other material filled with leaves, weeds, and garden trimmings. It can be two to eight feet tall and six inches to three feet in diameter and should be dug at least an inch into the ground for stability. (Compost piles filled with chunky garden waste can be built relatively high without risk of compaction, whereas piles containing mostly food scraps or lawn grass let in less air and may develop anaerobic conditions if they are taller than five feet.)

Blend your tower into the landscape by letting your favorite climbing plants scramble up the sides. As autumn approaches, install a simple mesh lid to keep rodents from nesting in the tower, and leave the contents to decompose over the winter. By spring, the bottom of the tower will be filled with earthy-smelling, rich compost. If you'd rather reuse materials from around the house to make a tower, consider stackable crates, old garbage cans that can be drilled with holes, or laundry hampers that already have built-in ventilation. Note: If the tower cannot be enclosed, don't use it to compost food scraps.

Bootstrap Compost in Boston collects kitchen scraps from residents and transports them by bicycle to compost sites. Later, subscribers receive a portion of the finished product.

Multitask. Another space-saving strategy is to make or buy a bench or other piece of garden furniture that can also hold compost. Just think—a place to relax and admire your hard work in the garden, while composting critters cultivate rich soil beneath you. On page 60 is a plan for building your own beautiful cedar bench, with a secret compost chamber under the seat.

Aim high. In dense cities like New York, many gardeners are taking to their balconies and roofs. Tumblers are a great option for rooftop spaces and balconies (see "Bins and Other Equipment," page 46). They are more effective than other bins at holding moisture and protecting compost from the drying effects of wind, heat, and direct sunlight, which become more pronounced the higher you climb in a building. Tumblers also keep compost microbes off the surface of the roof, where they can damage vulnerable surface materials. Consult with your building super or an architect to make sure your roof will hold the weight of a bin and if so, where it will be best supported—compost can be surprisingly heavy due to the high levels of moisture needed for decomposition.

Composting Communally

If you want to compost your food and garden waste but don't have the appropriate space or the time, resources, or inclination to do all the work yourself, take advantage of the growing number of community composting facilities available in many cities.

The scale of these efforts ranges from small, single-building projects to citywide programs. As the human population continues its shift to dense urban centers, sustainable waste-management solutions like these will become more and more necessary.

Shared Systems Make the best use of available space in your apartment building or neighborhood by sharing a compost structure with your neighbors. Find out whether there are any communal composting systems near your home, and if not, who might be amenable to starting one with you. Put up flyers in your building or around the neighborhood to garner interest. Take a composting class and hold a meeting to educate others in the maintenance of a group system. This way the cost and labor are shared, and you build community around compost!

Community Gardens Many city gardeners do all their composting communally. Some community gardens restrict the use of their composting systems to those who manage plots in the garden, but others act as neighborhood food-waste and leaf-processing centers, composting scraps and other organics from anyone interested in dropping them off. For example, in just one year, volunteers for Compost for Brooklyn—located in a tiny 20-by-12-foot lot in the neighborhood of Kensington—composted almost 20,000 pounds of local food waste and used the resulting compost to nurture a small garden of native plants and neighborhood street trees. Another community garden, 6/15 Green, in nearby Park Slope, has taken this a step further by offering a compost membership. Members commit six to eight hours of work each year to turn and maintain the commu-

Tackling the NIMBY Phenomenon

Though the benefits of composting are clear to its many devotees, some city dwellers are reluctant to welcome composting to their neighborhoods. Jon Pope of the Prospect Heights Community Farm, in Brooklyn, sums it up this way: "Compost is easy. People are hard." He and his colleagues have been composting at their community farm since the early 2000s, running a top-notch operation and providing a great service to their community—but they must still deal with worried neighbors as well as garden members who would prefer to use the compost space for garden beds.

Why would anyone want to thwart a responsible, sustainable habit like composting? Fears of bad odors and vermin plague the compost community, even though most well-managed composting operations and home bins have no such problems. The key to dealing with your neighbors' concerns is education. Provide them with information about the benefits and safe production of compost. Set up workshops or educational sessions where your neighbors can voice their doubts in an open environment. A simple tour of a healthy compost system might be enough to change many people's minds. And a gift of a plant potted up with compost might also help allay their fears—and perhaps even persuade them to start their own composting adventure.

Sheet Composting in Raised Beds

Sheet composting—also referred to as lasagna gardening—is an age-old technique often used to enlarge a perennial border or convert part of a lawn into a vegetable patch. In urban gardens faced with poor or contaminated soil, it's also a great way to fill a raised bed with a healthy growing medium for edibles. Heavy feeders like tomatoes and peppers will love this nutrient-rich garden. Autumn is a good time to begin due to the availability of fallen leaves, a key ingredient. Here's how to do it.

Build the frame. You can vary the dimensions to fit your space, but a four-by-eight-foot bed, two to three feet high, is typically a good size. If a soil test reveals lead or other contaminants, lay down a layer of landscape fabric to prevent roots from growing into the contaminated soil while allowing air and water flow. Be sure to use non-pressure-treated lumber.

Lay down your base. Begin with a layer of cardboard on the bottom of the bed, which will break down very slowly as it smothers weeds and soaks up moisture. Chop up some twigs, small branches, or hedge trimmings into one-inch pieces and layer them four inches thick over the cardboard—this will provide good drainage for the bed. Add an eight-inch layer of fallen leaves or straw, and then water your bed.

Continue adding layers. Next, lay down two inches of well-rotted manure or compost. Then add about four inches of grass clippings or other yard waste mixed with salad greens and coffee grounds. (Avoid adding other kitchen scraps, as these might attract rodents and other animals.) Cover this with a fluffy, eight-inch layer of leaves or straw. Then start all over again, layering brown materials, compost, and greens, until your bed is full. Water once more and leave it to decompose over the winter.

Prepare for planting. When spring is near, your bed will have shrunk in bulk; simply add more materials to fill it up again. Come planting time, add a six-inch layer of soil and plant your garden. A little organic fertilizer like blood meal or fish emulsion will give it a jump start, and water deeply.

Do it again! By the time you've harvested the last of your vegetables in fall, much of the organic matter will have decomposed, lowering the level significantly. To prepare your garden for the following year's planting, begin the process over again, omitting only the cardboard base.

nity piles and are allowed to take home finished compost. In one year alone, 6/15 Green provided over two tons of compost for member gardeners and neighborhood street trees.

Collection Programs As landfills run out of space and more and more city residents become concerned about the environmental impacts of landfilling garbage, municipal bodies and city-funded organizations have begun to think more constructively about composting urban organic waste. In the face of budget shortages or lack of government response, volunteer groups are also stepping in to provide solutions.

For example, in New York City, what started out as a small volunteer effort has expanded to a citywide, municipally funded collection program. The volunteer-run Fort Greene Compost Project in Brooklyn began to collect waste at the local farmers' market in 2005, taking it to participating community gardens for composting. In 2011, the project expanded into a city-funded program, coordinated by municipal and community partners, including the NYC Department of Sanitation and the nonprofit GrowNYC. Currently, there are sites at 25 city greenmarkets.

Elsewhere, bicycle-based kitchen-waste pickup services—such as the Pedal Co-op in Philadelphia and Bootstrap Compost in Boston—have also grown in popularity. Bootstrap Compost, for example, hauls away food scraps from Boston area homes and businesses for $8 a week and turns it into compost for use by local farms. Bootstrap subscribers also receive a portion of the finished compost for their gardens. Some cities, such as Milwaukee, provide residential yard waste pickup services as well as decentralized food-waste composting options.

Small, dense cities like Seattle, Portland, and San Francisco, as well as many county governments, have also created highly efficient residential organics-collection programs. The success of these programs depends on a number of factors, including local government commitment and funding, the ability to secure large swaths of land for compost processing, and education and outreach efforts to minimize contamination of the organics put out for collection. But because their residents are diverting so much material from the waste stream, some cities have been able to switch to biweekly garbage pickup for significant savings to their budgets, a plus for everyone. Hopefully, successful programs like these will be replicated and composting will become more widespread each year, just as curbside recycling grew in decades past.

Glossary
Niall Dunne

anaerobic Living without air. The decomposition of organic matter can be accomplished either by aerobic microorganisms that require oxygen or by anaerobic ones that function in the absence of oxygen. In composting, anaerobic decomposition is generally less desirable than aerobic because it's slower, produces foul-smelling sulfur-containing by-products, and results in the emission of methane, a powerful greenhouse gas. Regular turning helps maintain a porous compost pile, which increases oxygen levels and discourages anaerobic decomposition.

chelation Occurs in soil when metal ions, such as some plant nutrients, bind with certain organic molecules—abundant in humus—to form complexes known as chelates. In the case of plant nutrients, this process protects them from being leached out of the topsoil by rainwater and increases their availability for use by plants. Chelation can also bind up toxic metals such as lead and cadmium in soil, making them less available for absorption by plants. Adding compost to your soil increases the benefits of chelation to your plants by increasing humus.

clew A group of worms, such as that found in a vermicomposting bin.

compaction A type of soil degradation that occurs when the pore spaces in the soil collapse under the weight of machinery, foot traffic, or natural forces such as heavy rainfall, leading to the restriction of air and water flow to plant roots. One way to repair compacted soil is to add organic matter, especially compost, which helps rebuild soil structure and restore soil porosity.

compost A humus-rich soil conditioner, plant fertilizer, and garden mulch created by the decomposition of organic matter under controlled conditions.

compost tea A liquid extract made by steeping compost in water. When applied to plant leaves or root zones, compost tea acts as a source of readily available nutrients and may also help suppress certain plant diseases. Modern brewing techniques involve pumping air into the tea to nurture populations of beneficial bacteria, fungi, and other microorganisms. This is termed "actively aerated compost tea."

feedstock Any bulk raw material used as a main ingredient in a manufacturing process. Common feedstocks for the manufacture of compost include grass clippings, yard trimmings, and kitchen scraps.

hardware cloth A heavy-gauge wire mesh frequently used to line compost bins for rodent resistance.

humus Decomposed organic matter in soil that is "stable," or relatively resistant to further decay. Finished compost is made up mostly of humus. It improves soil structure and its ability to retain water. Though it is not a source of nutrients for plants, humus increases soil fertility by preventing nutrients from leaching out of the soil and by moderating soil pH, which makes nutrients more available to plants. Humus also helps your plants by binding up soil contaminants.

leachate Liquid that picks up particles or dissolved substances from the solids it flows through. Compost leachate that gathers at the bottom of a compost pile from excess moisture usually contains dissolved plant nutrients, but it may also contain products of anaerobic decomposition that can be harmful if added to your plants.

leaf mold Compost formed by the breakdown of leaves. It can take more than a year to make good-quality leaf mold. You can speed up the process somewhat by shredding the leaves before adding them to the pile, occasionally turning the pile, and keeping the material moist.

lignin A complex organic (carbon-based) compound that imparts mechanical strength to wood. A major precursor of humus, it is slow to decompose in nature and in the compost pile.

loam Soil in which the mineral particles—clay, silt, and sand—are of relatively even concentration. Loamy-textured soils that are rich in organic matter feel soft and crumbly and are the most desirable for gardening and farming, because they combine good aeration and drainage with good water and nutrient retention. Soils that are sandy or clayey can be improved through the addition of organic matter, especially compost.

mesophilic Thriving at moderate temperatures. In composting, this term refers to the initial and late (or curing) stages of the hot, aerobic process, when temperatures are relatively low, typically between 68°F and 113°F, and mesophilic microorganisms are predominant.

mulch A material spread on the surface of soil to prevent erosion, reduce evaporation, moderate soil temperature, and suppress weeds. Mulches can be inorganic (such as crushed stone, plastic, and crumb rubber) or organic (such as pine needles, nutshells, and compost). In most climates and situations, organic mulches are generally preferable because they are renewable and eventually biodegrade, enriching the soil. Lighter-textured composts, such as those made from leaves and yard waste, make effective mulches.

mycorrhizae Symbiotic relationships between fungi and plants via the plant root systems. The plants provide food for the fungi in the form of photosynthesized sugar;

the fungi help the plants by enhancing their ability to absorb water and nutrients. Compost made from the roots of plants may contain mycorrhizal fungi and can be applied to soil to increase populations.

soil A mixture of weathered mineral particles (sand, silt, and clay), organic matter, water, and air blanketing most of the earth's terrestrial surface. Good garden topsoil is roughly 45 percent mineral particles, 5 percent organic matter, 25 percent water, and 25 percent air by volume. Maintaining a balance of these components is important for the health of your soil and plants. Spreading compost on your soil every year is a good way to sustain or restore its organic matter. It also helps stabilize the pores in the soil, balancing air and water levels.

soil structure The way components of soil—clay, silt, sand, and organic matter particles—aggregate together. Good-quality soil has a granular or crumb structure, containing a balance of large pores that allow water to infiltrate, drain, and be replaced by air, and small pores that absorb and retain moisture. Adding organic matter such as compost to your soil is generally the best way to improve and maintain its structure.

thermophilic Thriving at high temperatures. In composting, this term refers to the middle stage of the hot, aerobic process, when temperatures rise above 113°F and thermophilic microorganisms predominate. This stage can last several weeks to months, depending on the size of the compost system. It's during this stage that heat-sensitive pathogens, fly larvae, and weed seeds in the compost are killed.

till To mechanically manipulate the soil. The objective of tilling the soil with a plow or rototiller is to improve its structure, or tilth. However, in the long-term, tillage—even when it involves the addition of compost or other organic matter—can damage soil structure and lead to compaction. Top-dressing (see below) garden beds with compost slowly improves soil structure without the risk of compaction.

tilth A term for describing the physical qualities or structure of soil (see "soil structure"). A soil that's "in good tilth" contains a balanced mix of water and air to nurture plants and beneficial soil organisms and is also easy to cultivate. Adding compost to a soil is a time-honored way of improving and maintaining its tilth.

top-dress To spread compost or other amendments on the surface of garden beds or lawn in order to enhance soil fertility, improve soil structure, and act as a protective mulch.

vermicompost Compost resulting from the breakdown of organic matter by earthworms in an enclosed bin or other controlled environment. Vermicompost is an excellent soil conditioner (for improving soil structure) and nutrient-rich organic fertilizer.

For More Information

FACT SHEETS AND FINDERS

FindAComposter.com
Directory of composting facilities throughout North America

U.S. Composting Council
compostingcouncil.org
Composting fact sheets and reports, state-by-state links to composting resources, searchable directory of compost facilities

U.S. Environmental Protection Agency "Composting at Home"
epa.gov/recycle/composting.html
Composting fact sheets aimed at the homeowner

WSU Whatcom County Extension Composting
whatcom.wsu.edu/ag/compost
Extensive list of publications on the basics of composting from Washington State University

COMPOSTING IN SCHOOLS

Cornell Composting
compost.css.cornell.edu
Cornell University's excellent resource on the science of composting, including a section for teachers and students

---

New York City Compost Resources

The **NYC Compost Project** was created by the NYC Department of Sanitation in 1993 to provide compost education and outreach to NYC residents, nonprofit organizations, and businesses and technical assistance to community-based compost operations. Funded and managed through the Department of Sanitation's Bureau of Waste Prevention, Reuse and Recycling, NYC Compost Project programs are carried out by Department-funded staff at host sites in each borough, including at Brooklyn Botanic Garden. In addition to online information resources (see nyc.gov/wasteless/compostproject), the NYC Compost Project offers

- Classes and workshops for individuals and institutions that address outdoor composting, indoor worm bin composting, and sustainable lawn care

- Master composter certification, a train-the-trainer program that includes intensive classroom instruction, field trips, and 30 hours of community outreach to help advance on-site composting in New York City

- Worm composting workshops for teachers, classroom worm bin visits, hands-on workshops for kids, and service-learning opportunities for students

- Compost demonstration sites in each borough

- Helplines and technical assistance, including answers to common questions, assistance building bins, and low-cost bins and worms

- Distribution of finished compost to residents for green-space improvement projects

To learn more about the NYC Compost Project in Brooklyn, email compost@bbg.org.

BINS AND SUPPLIES

Arbico Organics
arbico-organics.com
Composting tools and supplies, including bins, worm kits, and tea brewing systems

CompostBins.com
Huge selection of bins, tumblers, worm composters, and other supplies

Earthfort
earthfort.com
Compost tea brewing kits, additives, and information

Gardeners Supply Company
gardeners.com
A full range of composting equipment, from bins to thermometers

The Greenhouse Catalog
greenhousecatalog.com
Bins, compost aerators, worm bins, compost pails, and more

Instructables
instructables.com
DIY project sharing site that contains compost-related items including pallet bins and a drum sifter (see Trommel Compost Sifter project)

VERMICOMPOSTING

Earthworm Digest
wormdigest.org
A lively earthworm discussion forum

Find Worms
findworms.com
Locator for worm farms that sell composting worms in your area

Great Lakes Worm Watch
www.nrri.umn.edu/worms
Information on invasive earthworms

Lower East Side Ecology Center
lesecologycenter.org
Worms and other resources for New Yorkers

Uncle Jim's Worm Farm
unclejimswormfarm.com
Compost worms, kits, bins, and more

Worms Eat My Garbage
Mary Appelhof, Flower Press, 1997

COMPOSTABLE PRODUCTS

Biodegradable Products Institute
www.bpiworld.org
Nonprofit group that certifies commercially compostable products

Vinçotte OK Compost HOME
okcompost.be/en
Belgian organization that certifies products that break down in a home composting bin

FURTHER READING

The Complete Compost Gardening Guide
Barbara Pleasant and Deborah L. Martin, Storey Publishing, 2008

Healthy Soils for Sustainable Gardens
Niall Dunne, editor, Brooklyn Botanic Garden, 2009

Let It Rot!
Stu Campbell, Storey Publishing, 2008

The Nature and Properties of Soils
Nyle C. Brady and Ray R. Weil, Prentice Hall, 2007

Organic Gardener's Composting
Steve Solomon, Aeterna, 2011

The Rodale Book of Composting
Grace Gershuny and Deborah L. Martin, editors, Rodale Press, 1992

Teaming with Microbes
Jeff Lowefels and Wayne Lewis, Timber Press, 2010

Contributors

Jenny Blackwell is project manager for the NYC Compost Project in Brooklyn, based at Brooklyn Botanic Garden. An advocate of community-based composting, she is passionate about strengthening local resources for New Yorkers and developing soil remediation programs for urban areas.

Joshua Cohen is a former project manager for the NYC Compost Project in Brooklyn. He currently specializes in environmental philanthropy and has worked on advocacy campaigns and research projects for universities, government agencies, NGOs, and the private sector. He lives in Brooklyn.

Niall Dunne is a former staff editor at BBG and the editor of the BBG handbooks *A Native Plants Reader* (2012), *Great Natives for Tough Places* (2009), and *Healthy Soils for Sustainable Gardens* (2009). He lives in Seattle, where he manages publications for Washington Park Arboretum and happily contributes his food and yard waste to the city's curbside collection and composting program.

Ashley Gamell manages BBG's Discovery Garden, a hands-on learning garden where children explore the plant world and dig enthusiastically for red wigglers around a giant outdoor worm bin. A plant educator and horticulturist at BBG since 2006, she is also a plant-inspired poet.

Elizabeth Peters is the director of Digital and Print Media at BBG, where she oversees the Guides for a Greener Planet imprint, bbg.org, and other digital initiatives. She composts at a community garden in Brooklyn.

Jon Pope is a Brooklyn-based builder, LEED-accredited professional, and certified master composter who has designed and built compost systems for community gardens. He was awarded the GreenBridge Green Neighbor Award in 2009.

Christopher Roddick is an ISA-certified arborist at BBG, where he uses compost tea and other sustainable practices. He wrote (with Beth Hanson) the BBG handbook *The Tree Care Primer* (2007) and contributed to *Healthy Soils for Sustainable Gardens* (2009).

CONTRIBUTORS TO THE PREVIOUS EDITION

Mary Appelhof wrote *Worms Eat My Garbage* as well as numerous articles on solid-waste topics. A biologist and educator from Kalamazoo, Michigan, Appelhof founded Flowerfield Enterprises, a vermicomposting supply company.

Grace Gershuny is the author of several books and articles on soil management and composting, including *Start with the Soil*, published in 1997 by Rodale. She serves on the board of the Highfields Center for Composting in Hardwick, Vermont.

Benjamin Grant is a former instructor at BBG, where he taught courses in composting and environmental issues to children, adults, and landscape professionals.

Beth Hanson is a former managing editor of Brooklyn Botanic Garden's handbook series and served as lead editor for the 1997 edition of *Easy Compost*. She writes about gardening, science, and health for various publications, including *Organic Gardening* magazine. She lives outside New York City, where she is a master gardener volunteer.

Patricia Jasaitis is a former coordinator of BBG's Urban Composting Project. She has also worked in community gardening with the Green Guerrillas in Manhattan and in urban forestry at the Morris Arboretum in Philadelphia.

Joseph Keyser is president of GreenMan Communications, host of the *GreenMan Show*, and the first winner of the Composting Council's H. Clark Gregory Award.

Miranda Smith wrote many books on gardening, including *Your Backyard Herb Garden* (1997) and *Backyard Fruits and Berries* (1994), both published by Rodale. She taught organic horticulture and farming at the New England Small Farm Institute.

Rod Tyler, a former vice president of the Composting Council and member of the council's marketing committee, has written dozens of articles about compost.

PHOTOS

Laura Berman cover, pages 6, 9, 18, 38, 39, 43, 52, 80 (left), 82, 83, 84

Jennifer Blackwell pages 22, 25, 39, 40, 49 (middle left), 75

Nina Browne page 34

Walter Chandoha page 27

Emily-Bell Dinan pages 2, 20, 36, 72, 95

Jean-Marc Grambert page 76

Colleen Grant page 21

Bill Johnson page 12 (lower right)

Uli Lorimer page 14

Tien Mao page 67 (6)

Jonathan McCurdy page 96

Maureen O'Brien page 90

Elizabeth Peters pages 4, 31, 32, 33, 35, 50, 54, 58 (bottom), 61 (4), 62 (6)

Sarah Schmidt pages 49 (top right, middle right, lower right), 80 (right), 92

Tara Thayer pages 46, 49 (top left, lower left), 57 (6), 58 (top left, top right), 64, 88

Brian Valentine page 12 (all but lower right)

ILLUSTRATIONS

Elizabeth Ennis pages 15, 16

Manny Jose pages 29, 44, 70, 71, 85, 98

Gregory Nemac pages 55, 60

Index

testing compost readiness, 40, 77, 78
Glossary, 100–102
Grass clippings, 20, 23, 26. *See also* Herbaceous trimmings
Greens. *See* Browns and greens

H

Hardware cloth, defined, 100
Herbaceous trimmings, 21–22
Hot composting. *See* Fast/hot composting
Household materials, 22
Humus, 7, 9, 11, 19, 101

I

Indoor vermicomposting, 31, 65–71. *See also* Worm bins
    assembling system, 69
    choosing bedding, 66
    collecting, using castings, 70
    defined, 65, 102
    feeding worms, 69
    invasive worms and, 71
    maintaining bins, 69–70
    making/buying bin, 65
    materials for, 65
    moisture management, 68, 69
    resources, 104
    sharing extra worms, 69–70
    system capacity, 65
    troubleshooting worm bins, 68
    worms for, 66–68
Inoculating soil, 17
Invasive worms, 71

L

Leachate, defined, 101
Leaf mold, 19, 66, 101
Leaves
C:N ratio, 23–25
    composting, 19, 26
    greens, browns and, 25
    as mulch, 26
    sheet composting, 43, 98
    shredding, 52

sourcing, 94
Lignin, 17, 101
Lime, pH and, 45
Loam, 66, 101
Lumbricus rubellus, 66, 71
Lumbricus terrestris, 69

M

Managing systems, 39–43, 69–70
Manures
    to avoid, 23, 24
    compostable, 23, 24
    of worms. *See* Indoor vermicomposting; Worm bins; Worms
Materials, compostable. *See also* Browns and greens
    agricultural manures, 23
    compostable plastics and, 29
    food scraps, 20–21, 23, 53. *See also* Indoor vermicomposting
    grass, 20, 26
    herbaceous trimmings, 21–22
    household materials, 22
    leaves, 19, 26
    woody materials, 21
Mesh/wire bins, adjustable, 48, 49
Mesophilic phase, 15, 101
Microbes, 7, 11, 14, 15, 17, 25–26, 27, 87, 88
Millipedes, 13, 16
Mites, 13, 16
Mixing compost. *See* Turning compost
Modified trash can, 49, 50
Moisture levels
    composting, 25–26, 38
    worm bin, 68, 69
Mowers, mulching, 53
Mulch
    compost as, 79–80, 89
    defined, 101
    leaves as, 26
Mulching mowers, 53

Mycorrhizae, 11, 101
Myths debunked, 44–45

N

Nematodes, 16, 87
New York City resources, 103
Nitrogen (N)
    carbon-to-, ratios, 23–25, 44
    cold composting and, 28
    commercial fertilizer and, 45, 80
    compostable materials providing, 19, 20, 22, 23, 94
    decomposition and, 14, 25, 41, 45
    excess, 8, 11, 25, 41
    hot composting and, 27
    increasing, 45
    insufficient, 41
    levels in compost, 8
    unfinished compost robbing, 77, 82–83
Nutrients. *See also specific nutrients*
    in compost, 80–82
    compost holding for plants, 9–10
    pH and, 10–11

P

Pails, collection, 53
Pesticide-treated plants, 23
Pests
    avoiding in compost, 20–21, 23, 24, 37, 42, 69, 71, 89
    compost bench and, 63
    compost fighting, 11
    compost harboring, myth debunked, 44
    rodent-proofing piles, 32, 93–94
    troubleshooting (in compost), 42
Phases, composting, 15–17
Phosphorus (P), 8, 10, 11, 80, 85

composting, 41–42
worm bins, 68
Tumblers, 49, 51, 96
Turning compost
aerating tools and, 51
bins simplifying, 38, 48, 50,
51
hot piles, 27
importance of, 25–26
moisture, air and, 25–26,
39–40
solving problems by, 41,
42, 68
Two-bin composter, building,
54, 55–59

U
Urban areas. *See* City,
composting in; Indoor
vermicomposting; Worm bins

V
Vermicomposting. *See* Indoor
vermicomposting

W
Waste
collection programs, 99
compostable. *See* Materials,
compostable
exploring sustainability and,
74–75
worm bins and, 74–75
yard, composting options, 26
Weeds. *See* Herbaceous
trimmings
Windrows, 35
Wire bins, adjustable, 48, 49
Wooden bins, slatted, 48–49
Woody materials, 21, 23, 26

Worm bins. *See also* Indoor
vermicomposting
in classroom, 73–75
ecosystem lessons, 74
exploring waste and
sustainability, 74–75
problem-solving lessons with,
75
setting up, 73
students helping manage,
73–74
Worms
extra, sharing, 69–70
feeding, 69
invasive, nonbeneficial, 71

Y
Yard waste, composting options,
26

Guides for a Greener Planet

A Native Plants Reader

Community Gardening

Healthy Soils for Sustainable Gardens

Gardening With Children

Edible Gardens

Fragrant Designs

The Wildlife Gardener's Guide

The Climate Conscious Gardener

Green Roofs and Rooftop Gardens

Promoting Organic and Sustainable Gardening

Brooklyn Botanic Garden's award-winning guides provide expert advice in a practical, compact format. To order other fine titles, visit bbg.org/handbooks. Learn more about Brooklyn Botanic Garden at bbg.org.